GUTS

Find Your Greatness, Beat the Odds, Live From Passion

SAM BRACKEN

Bestselling Author of *My Orange Duffel Bag*

Other Books by Sam Bracken

- *My Orange Duffel Bag: A Journey to Radical Change*

- *My Roadmap: A Personal Guide to Balance, Power, and Purpose*

- *Unwind! 7 Principles for a Stress-Free Life, with Michael Olpin*

GUTS

Find Your Greatness, Beat The Odds, Live From Passion

Sam Bracken

First edition published by Mango Publishing Group.
Cover Design: Roberto Núñez
Design and Layout: Laura Mejía
Author Photo: Kevin Garrett

For permission requests, please contact the publisher at:

Mango Publishing Group

2850 Douglas Road, 3rd Floor

Coral Gables, FL 33134 USA

info@mango.bz

For special orders, quantity sales, course adoptions and corporate sales, please email the publisher at sales@mango.bz. For trade and wholesale sales, please contact Ingram Publisher Services at customer.service@ingramcontent.com or +1.800.509.4887.

Library of Congress Cataloging

Names: Bracken, Sam
Title: GUTS / by Sam Bracken
Library of Congress Control Number: 2016918138
ISBN 9781633534759 (paperback), ISBN 9781633534766 (eBook)
BISAC Category Code: SEL027000 SELF-HELP / Personal Growth / Success
GUTS: *Find Your Greatness, Beat the Odds, Live From Passion*
ISBN: 978-1-63353-475-9

Printed in the United States of America

This book is dedicated to Isaiah Beaumont Bracken, my wonderful firstborn son. Beau, I love you with all my head, heart, and GUTs. You have endured much in your life, yet you still move forward, working through your challenges with great courage, tenacity, purpose, passion and most of all with GUTs. Your heart is pure and good. I have seen you grow through amazing challenges to become a great man. Thank you for the hero you are and the even greater hero you will become.

"
Sam Bracken is one of the most passionate, inspiring, engaging writers and speakers that I know. GUTs will be another classic that helps people enable greatness in their lives! **"**

Mark Josie
General Manager East Region, FranklinCovey

"
GUTs is a courageous book that invites us to move beyond living a safe life toward living an exciting, fulfilling life; to function at a higher level, focusing not only on our mind and heart, but also our intuition. In this book, Sam Bracken shows us how. **"**

Dr. Michael Olin

"
Sam has done it again, GUTs typifies his core, his character and the passion by which he lives. Sam from his childhood was forced through no fault of his own to make hard choices under extreme circumstances. That takes GUTs! When it comes to excuses, Sam simply does not know the meaning of that word. **"**

Luther Perkins
Executive Coach and Consultant

"
I've spent 30 years helping people learn to have "Crucial Conversations." Sam's book is about the most crucial conversation you will ever have—the one you have with yourself. We all have a voice deep down inside of us—down in the GUT—a guiding voice that can let you know if you're doing what's right in your life. This book will help you prosper by connecting with that ennobling voice. **"**

Joseph Grenny
New York Times bestselling author

"
Your GUT very rarely leads you down a wrong path, yet going with your GUT can be the toughest choice to make because it makes you live outside your comfort zone. It takes real GUTs to live your life from your place of passion. Sam has hit the nail on the head with this book, giving all who read it a path to find and reach their own personal greatness regardless of their circumstances. **"**

M. Todd Stansbury
VP and Director of Athletics at Georgia Institute of Technology

"
Pain, discouragement, struggle, and failure are no strangers to Sam Bracken. What makes Sam different is his ability to pick himself up and not let bitterness and regret hold him back from learning and moving forward. Throughout his life, Sam has had the GUTs to let his trials refine him rather than define him. As an author and mentor, Sam gives hope and inspiration to anyone needing help turning failure into success. **"**

Carine Clark
CEO & President at MaritzCX

"

Sam has taken himself from the worst of struggles to become one of our society's greatest leaders and most inspiring authors. He is definitely a living example of what it truly means to have GUTs. A must read for everyone!

"

Shea Sealy
Business Founder & Entrepreneur

"

Many in the field of motivation talk about personal resolve, proactive choice, determination, and grit. I call this the blah, blah, blah…it's just talk! In Sam's book GUTs, he gives us his personal life experiences to help anyone understand how to overcome obstacles, set a big vision, and define a life of purpose greater than self. He teaches how anyone can reach deep inside and develop a clear path that inspires love, GUTs, and the will to achieve success.

"

Michael K. Simpson
CEO of Simpson Executive Coaching and Author of *Unlocking Potential and Your Seeds of Greatness*

"

As a former college quarterback myself, I know how tough it is to make the team, even with plenty of advantages. Sam Bracken had no advantages, but he went from being a hopeless street kid to a champion college football player. In this insightful book, he illustrates how success in life is less about talent, wealth, or good luck, and more about GUTs. And having GUTs is a choice anyone can make!

"

Sean Covey
author of *The 7 Habits of Highly Effective Teens* and *The 6 Most Important Decisions You'll Ever Make: A Guide for Teens*

" It takes GUTs to spill your GUTs in a book and then to share it with the world. I can't think of a better title or subject for Sam to write about. He is the subject matter expert on what it takes to succeed in every way considering the challenges he faced as a youth. Sam is actually proud of his upbringing—it made him the man he is today. I highly recommend this book to everyone who wants to prove that they have the GUTs to succeed. **"**

Annie Oswald
Global Director Media Publishing at FranklinCovey Co.

" Few books excite me quite like my friend Sam Bracken's book, GUTs ! Full of passion and purpose, Sam's writing reveals his own personal journey to self-discovery, which both inspires and educates tremendously. Yet the main focus of this work stems from the ardent teaching of something Sam truly believes in and is passionate about-learning how to dig deep and listen to your GUT in all that life offers you. This book is for anyone who wants to lose their baggage, find their purpose, and then vehemently pursue it! Definitely a GUTsy read! **"**

Stephen M. R. Covey
#1 bestselling author of *The Speed of Trust* and
coauthor of *Smart Trust*

" I spent five years with Sam Bracken at a time of transformation for him. His is a stunning story of courage, resiliency, and servant-leadership. We would all do well to read and heed his powerful message. **"**

Bill Curry
NCAA football coach and former NFL player

" For everyone who wants to leave their baggage
behind once and for all! **"**

Stephen R. Covey
author of *The 7 Habits of Highly Effective People*

" GUTs puts our 'decision-making processes' into perspective
like never before. Sam's down-to-earth writing is easy to
understand and I couldn't wait to learn more. He not only
explains what it means to have GUTs, but he explains why
we don't use them and how we can learn to. His courage to
use his GUTs to overcome his life struggles and to strengthen
others is so admirable. **"**

Donna Foster
author, keynote speaker and trainer

" Sam Bracken followed his gut to a very successful life. As a
close, personal friend for over 30 years, I can attest that his
experience is a testimony of truth that all of us can follow. The
lessons in GUTS can be applied to health, wealth, love and
happiness. The pillars for a successful life! **"**

Johnny Porter
Executive Vice President at CBRE, Inc.

"

Sam Bracken's message in GUTs is both poignantly personal and powerfully universal. He illustrates the great truth that every individual has greatness within, but that each of us must take personal responsibility for our lives. Sam provides a framework that, when acted on with courage and determination, will bring remarkable results. **"**

Shawn D. Moon
Executive Vice President, FranklinCovey

"

GUTs is an inspiring book which helps you tap into your life's passion, purpose and intuition so you are able to LOVE the life you live! It gives a new perspective in accomplishing your dreams as well as honoring others who do the same. This book will be a rewarding experience for all who read it! **"**

Crystal Nyman
Blue Diamond Wellness Advocate for Doterra Essential Oils

"

Sam's storytelling will engage you from the very first sentence and challenge you to become a better version of yourself, reach new levels, and live your unique purpose. This is a must read for anyone who has heard that inner voice to change, but can't seem to make it happen! **"**

Patrick Leddin Ph.D.
Associate Professor Managerial Studies Vanderbilt University and author of *Oliver's Spot*

"

In the business world there are many decisions that have to be made with very limited time to make them. Sam maps out a clear program that allows the reader to understand the purest way to make a decision. "

Ty Foster
motivational speaker and author of *Navigate to Greatness*

"

Are you ready to be moved toward greatness? Read this book! Inspiring and authentic! If Sam can move from tragedy to forgiveness, success, and incredibly positive influence, maybe you and I can. Thanks to Bracken, we can all have GUTs and the success that follows.

In this selfie-driven, blame-everyone-else culture, Bracken puts the responsibility for change and success on the only place that matters—one's self! But he does not leave you alone. He gives you the inspiration and tools to move forward powerfully in the right direction! "

David Horsage
author and speaker

TABLE OF CONTENTS

FOREWORD

By Bill Curry

Along with faith and love for my family, the capacity to endure that which must be endured is one of the underpinnings of my life.

Sam Bracken embodies that kind of endurance as well as anyone I've ever known. Long before I met him as his football coach at Georgia Tech, he knew how to GUT out the hard things in life. Long before he had all the supporting mechanisms of coaches, teachers, and counselors around him to help him, he developed that greatness of spirit that comes from deep down inside—from conquering massive life challenges with determination and joy.

As a youth, Sam overcame trials that would knock most of us down for good. He grew up on the fringes of a criminal gang, neglected, abused, and repeatedly abandoned. Drugs and alcohol were constants in his life. But even as a child, something in his GUT told him that kind of life was not for him; with no advantages except personal strength and discipline, he excelled in sports. So when he came to play at Tech, he already had a lot to teach the rest of us about having *GUTS*.

I used to teach at Baylor, a venerable school in Chattanooga, Tennessee, where the motto is *Magnanimitas*—Latin for "greatness of spirit." At Baylor, we learned that you don't become the person you're meant to be until you locate *magnanimitas* in yourself. I believe this is what Sam means by GUTs.

Let me explain. As an athlete, I was a very late bloomer. I was not a starting player until the fourth game of my fourth year. I had not pushed myself. But then at the end of a hard-fought bowl game in which my teammates were giving their all, I realized to my shame that *my jersey was still clean*! Suddenly I felt so embarrassed that I decided that would never happen again. I got busy, and with the help of one of my great coaches, John Robert Bell, I got into the weight room and worked and worked until I experienced that feeling that Sam talks about in this book—the deep-down joy of GUTting it out the very best you possibly can.

In the end, I barely made the NFL draft. Shockingly, the Green Bay Packers took me. Apparently, Vince Lombardi, the legendary coach of that legendary team, had worked all night to pick nineteen new players, and, exhausted, told his staff to do "something humorous" with the twentieth pick. I was that "humorous" selection.

So when I went to try out for the Packers as an undersized center, they told me to go block Ray Nitschke, one of the toughest linebackers who ever played the game of football. Nitschke was so tough that he not only survived when the wind blew over a gigantic steel coaching tower on him, he got up and kept playing. And I was supposed to block this guy.

Well, on my first try he broke my face mask and my nose and knocked me out. I had to decide if I was going to try again. Deep down, I couldn't stand to get cut from the Packers, so I hit him again and again and broke one helmet after another. My GUT said, "Either block him or kill yourself." But because of that kind of resolution (and because Lombardi was always watching), I eventually succeeded as a team player. I was never a Ray Nitschke, but I think I became the greatest player Bill Curry was capable of being.

The ironic thing is that I loved the grind. When you lie utterly exhausted and victorious on the field, all the pain and agony seems like a very small price to pay. Likewise, when a woman gives birth, the unspeakable pain and the joy can't be separated: once she sees the baby it's all worth it. That's GUTs. It is all about the extreme joy of giving your all and experiencing that personal victory.

If you have GUTs, after a while you get used to the pain. You know you're going to excel. When you beat your personal best, it's a heady thing—there's a chemical reaction in the body, a "high" you can't get any other way.

The people who do what Sam did come to love the grind. The people who can't bring themselves to love that part of it never really join the team. They never experience the joy of the team, where every single person pays the price.

Sam Bracken understands GUTs. He didn't come from where I did—from a nice suburban home with a supportive mom and dad. Unlike so many, Sam's scholarship didn't come easy—he got it because he truly deserved it. I love Sam and respect him as much as anyone I've ever known, partly because he taught me so much about what it means to have GUTs.

This book can be a source of hope and inspiration for everyone who faces great challenges in life — and who doesn't?. It teaches the truth—that real joy in life comes from doing the hard things, from listening to your GUT and loving the labor of becoming the best person you can be.

Bill Curry is a legend in the world of football. He was head coach at some of the greatest football schools in America—Georgia Tech, the University of Alabama, the University of Kentucky, and finally Georgia State. He played for Georgia Tech and then went for ten seasons with the Green Bay Packers, the Baltimore Colts, the Houston Oilers, and the Los Angeles Rams. Widely lauded for his integrity and wisdom, Bill Curry, the author of Ten Men You Meet in the Huddle, considers his players his beloved "boys." He says, "The greatest thing in my life after my family is my boys."

INTRODUCTION

GUTS!
A Few Thoughts to Start With...

I grew up the child of a rape, abused by a mobster stepfather and a sadistic older brother. My mom suffered a mental breakdown and abandoned me repeatedly. I was set on fire, used as a human dart board, molested sexually, and hooked on alcohol and drugs—all by age nine!

When I was twenty years old, after overcoming years of suffering, abuse, and neglect, my therapist asked me, "Sam, you should be dead, insane, or in prison, but you're not. Why?"

She couldn't figure out what made me grateful for my struggles. She couldn't imagine how I could have survived the horrors of my childhood, not to mention how I managed to thrive in spite of it all. She didn't understand why I was so driven to excel, improve, and grow, making the best out of every situation.

I explained to her two secrets that had made all the difference in my life.

The first was my ability to listen, understand, and respond to my GUT feelings, my intuition that my life was more than living in the dirt. There was something in me, something very deep down, telling me that my life had purpose and meaning beyond anything

23

I could imagine—and that I had the GUTs to "go" after it. Every disappointment, every challenge, and the massive struggles I have experienced—all of it fills my soul with gratitude.

The second was the handful of powerful, positive people—my "personal huddle"—who saw things in me I didn't even see in myself. In football, we huddle before each play. In the huddle we use everybody's strengths to the maximum. We call the play so everyone knows who's going to do what. I've decided that everybody needs a "personal huddle" of people they can count on for help. In my case, the members of my personal huddle reached out, reached across, and reached up to help me—just one kid. They loved me for no good reason and taught me how to change and how to build a clear vision of the future, discover a powerful purpose, achieve goals, and make everything work for my good.

Everybody falls in the dirt sometime. So how do we rise up from the dirt and win the race? Every person on this planet struggles with pain and discouragement. But not every person becomes better because of their challenges. Many folks spend their days "bitter"—pissed off and with a huge chip on their shoulder. Two people can go through exactly the same situation or circumstance, and one will learn from it, gain empathy from it, make course corrections because of it and become better; while the other lets it fester, constantly dwells on their disappointments, gets angry, and holds on to their victim status like a priceless artifact. Their life is filled with misery and pain.

Now, we hear all the time from well-meaning people, "Just let it go. Be better, not bitter."

Good advice, but no one tells you how to do it.

So I wrote this book. From my own experience, I hope to share with you how to "GUT it out" and fulfill your own great purposes in life.

I have heard it said that we become a reflection of our life's experiences. Fortunately for me, I've been able to rise up out of some significant setbacks early in my life. I still carry the challenges of my past, but today they are not heavy. I draw strength from my struggles. They are a gift to me—a gift of inspiration, strength, and empathy to light my path and help others on theirs.

So I "GUTted it out." Despite being homeless, I graduated high school with a 3.9 GPA and won a full-ride football scholarship to Georgia Institute of Technology. When I left my native Las Vegas for Atlanta, everything I owned fit in an orange duffel bag. Today I have a great family, an MBA, and a top executive job. I give speeches to tens of thousands of people each year, from CEOs of big companies to convicts in federal prison. I found my purpose, and I have loved each step I've taken along the way.

"Gold medals aren't really made of gold. They're made of sweat, determination, and a hard-to-find alloy called GUTs."

-Dan Gable, Olympic gold medal wrestler

What is *your* great purpose? What do you love to do? What great contributions will you make? How can you leverage your head, your heart, and your GUTs and strive in joy and success without the grinding drudgery of struggle without vision and purpose?

It's the question of a lifetime. How is it that some people are defeated by life even when they show a lot of grit? They strain and fight and labor and toil but experience no joy: "I hate this job/this town/this school/this family/this life." They fantasize about a life without stress or effort or pain.

Then there are other people who work just as hard if not harder, exerting themselves to the utmost but loving every minute of it. They feel pain just like anyone else, but sometimes they don't even seem to notice it. They too serve and struggle and sacrifice, but they relish all of it.

The difference? *These people have GUTS!* "Why me?" doesn't occur to them. They focus on what they should do to make things better. A life without stress or pain would be meaningless to them. They don't fantasize about a life without effort because it would be a throwaway life.

Anything worth doing takes GUTs. Anything I give a damn about takes GUTs. It takes GUTs to *choose* to stand up, to declare yourself, to begin a new life, to become a change agent, to be "the tipping point," to "turn the ship around."

It takes GUTs to choose a *meaningful* life. It takes GUTs to leave a so-so job and go for your passion. It takes GUTs to love someone, to start a family, to commit your life to that love—and to stick to your commitment. It takes GUTs to make a difference in this world.

It takes GUTs for the addict to ask for help. It takes GUTs for the sexual assault survivor to name her accuser. It takes GUTs for a victim of domestic abuse to say "no more" and leave an abusive partner. It takes GUTs to stand up for what you believe in. You can have smarts and heartfelt commitment, but when you stand on the edge of the decision, it takes GUTs to make that leap.

Anyone can have GUTs. Anyone can have that single moment in time where everything changes. It doesn't take special knowledge, it doesn't take time: it takes a *calculated* pause in decision making and it takes listening to what your GUT is telling you. It's not blind or reckless courage. It's knowing it's not going to be easy or comfortable or even popular at times, but it's going to make a big difference. It's going to be the right thing. And it's going to be *fantastic*!

In one moment, after a long hard day with tired feet and a heavy heart, Rosa Parks made a GUT decision in the face of certain consequences. She decided she would not give up her seat on the bus to a white man. In that single moment of time, in a single decision, she changed history—all because she had GUTs.

Knowledge gets us to the point of decision. The heart makes us care. *But the GUT tells us "Now is the moment of action!"*

In this book, I want to show you how to develop the GUTs to fulfill your own great purpose in life. From business executives trying to hit the must-reach numbers to people trying to lose weight, everybody knows it is one thing to have a strong sense of purpose in life, but achieving it is an entirely different story. It takes GUTs—tenacity, excitement, and strong "GUTsy" decisions. In this book you will learn how to actually get there—to fulfill your life's purpose with energy, determination, and *pure joy*.

PART 1

Go with your GUT

Discovering how to live in your place of passion: Your GUT Instincts!

CHAPTER 1

What is your GUT telling you?

What clear, unmistakable message is coming from deep down inside you? It's telling you about the passion and purpose you should be living for. You don't have to ask what you should be doing with your life—from the bottom of your being, you know.

On one of those spring days when it's not quite warm enough yet, a young man was chopping wood. The sun would heat him up and then dip behind a cloud to leave him chilled. He swung a big axe in a motion that was both easy and hard—it was a natural stroke, a practiced stroke.

The woodcutter had been doing this for hours, and he wouldn't be finished for hours to come. Tomorrow would be the same, and the day after and the day after. Most people would probably hate this kind of work. It was tough, dirty, monotonous, and even dangerous.

But he loved it.

Why?

That's the question the poet Robert Frost tried to answer as he told this story in his poem "Two Tramps in Mud Time"[1]:

> Good blocks of oak it was I split,
> As large around as the chopping block;
> And every piece I squarely hit
> Fell splinterless as a cloven rock.

It delighted the woodcutter to hit every single block of wood "squarely" so it would split clean. He was proud that there were no splinters. It not only takes skill to do this every time, but also the desire to do it. He did it right because it *mattered* to him.

> You'd think I never had felt before
> The weight of an ax-head poised aloft,
> The grip of earth on outspread feet,
> The life of muscles rocking soft
> And smooth and moist in vernal heat.

Every stroke of the axe was like the very first stroke he ever made. You hear about love at first sight, or the musician who first hears a piano, or the airplane pilot who solos for the first time. For this young woodcutter, just the feeling of the axe, the earth under his feet, and his own "rocking muscles" made him happy.

> My object in living is to unite
> My avocation and my vocation
> As my two eyes make one in sight.
> Only where love and need are one,
> And *the work is play* for mortal stakes,
> Is the deed ever really done
> For Heaven and the future's sakes.

The woodcutter knows an important truth: That a life well lived is all about "uniting avocation with vocation." What does that mean?

Well, it doesn't make sense at first, because an *avocation* is something you do outside of your *vocation*. You do it for fun, like

---

1 Frost, Robert, "Two Tramps in Mud Time," The Poetry of Robert Frost: The Collected Poems, Complete and Unabridged, ed. Edward Connery Letham, MacMillan, 2002, 275-276.

tennis, painting, or Sudoku. On the other hand, your vocation is serious. It's a job, a career, a profession. So how can you "unite" a vocation and an avocation?

Don't think I'm suggesting that you do Sudoku for a living or become a tennis pro (although real people really do those things). I think Frost is talking about connecting what you love deep down inside with what the world needs: "Only where love and need are one, and the work is play, is the deed ever really done."

He's saying that when your work and your play are the same thing, you start making a *life* instead of just making a *living*.

"No price is too high to pay for the privilege of owning yourself."

– Friedrich Nietzsche

There's something about chopping wood that appeals to the woodcutter. *His work is his play.* Nobody knows why he likes it so much—he just does. It's not something he ever thought about or planned for. He's just always done it and longs to keep doing it. When he's away from it, he wants to get back to it. When he's chopping, he doesn't want to stop.

This woodcutter makes no sense to most of us. The *Wall Street Journal* says logging is the worst of the "3D" jobs ("Dirty, Dangerous, and Difficult")[2]. You and I might think he's crazy, but it's none of our business. His desire to be a woodcutter comes from somewhere deep inside him. It comes from his GUT!

Let's find out if you're a person with GUTs. Take this little quiz. When you're finished, add up your points and read the key to find out if you have GUTs.

---

2 "Career and Job News," Wall Street Journal, September 12, 2010.
http://www.careerjournal.com/jobhunting/change/20020507-lee.html

DO YOU HAVE GUTS?

True or false?

1. Gutsy people don't quit when pursuing their passion.

2. To be "gutsy" is to be humble.

3. Risky behavior takes guts.

4. A person with guts doesn't walk away from a fight.

5. It takes guts to be gentle and kind.

6. Gutsy people are happy.

7. Real joy comes from doing hard, painful things.

8. Gutsy work is risky work, like firefighting or driving race cars.

9. It takes guts to show love to others.

10. Gutsy people quit when there's no point to continuing.

    I am 1) Not likely   2) Pretty unlikely 3) Could go one way or the other 4) Pretty likely   5) Very likely to do the following:

11. Tell the truth even if it makes me look bad.

12. Apologize if I do something that hurts someone.

13. Admit it when I make a mistake.

14. Keep my promises.

15. Stand up for someone who is being attacked verbally or physically.

16. Trust people until I see a reason not to.

17. Take responsibility whether the outcome is good or bad.

18. Refuse to do work that isn't important.

19. Walk my talk.

20. Take other people's opinions seriously.

Take 5 points for each correct true or false answer for questions 1-10. Key: 1T 2T 3F 4F 5T 6T 7T 8F 9T 10T

Enter your score here: _____

If your score is...	Then...
91-100	You understand what it really means to have GUTs. You almost always do the right thing, the often hard but honest thing—and that takes more GUTs than anything else in life. Your GUT can tell you what the right thing is in most situations, so keep listening to your GUT.
81-90	You're unclear on what it means to have GUTs, but you have a pretty good instinct anyway for doing what's right. Humility, kindness, honesty, following your true passion—those things take GUTs.
71-80	You're confused about what it means to have GUTs. To be GUTsy is not about fighting or doing dangerous stuff. It's about being genuine, honest, keeping your commitments, and doing the right thing—that takes GUTs.
0-70	No GUTs. Gutless people don't respect themselves or others enough to do what's right and honest and kind. If that describes you, read this book carefully and take it to heart—or you're not likely to find success in your life.

What does your score mean?

To really understand what it means to have GUTs, let me tell you the story of my friend Kyle Bjornstad. He's a nice, ordinary guy in most ways, and a good but not spectacular athlete. He could be any one of us. But in my book (this book, actually), he's one of the greatest men I've ever known in my life. If anyone has GUTs, Kyle does.

Even as a little kid, Kyle had a passion for basketball and a fixation on playing for the great Oregon State University (OSU), a Division I school with a venerable basketball tradition going back to the 1920s.

"I loved Oregon State from the time I could walk. My family lives in Eugene, home of the rival University of Oregon Ducks. My dad even worked for the Ducks. But for me, it was never a matter of what I wanted to do or where I wanted to go: I was going to play basketball for Oregon State.

"All the odds were against me, and I knew it. Full grown, I was only a five-foot-ten white kid, a good player but not great. But I was obsessed. It was in my GUT. In high school I never went partying or anything—I was always at the gym late at night or under the bridge playing pick-up ball with anyone I could find.

"At fifteen, I was looking forward to playing on the high school team as a junior. But just before school started, I was playing in a dumb summer-league game that meant nothing—and I tore a ligament in my knee. I was devastated. I had to sit out the whole basketball season.

"For months I worked like crazy to get my knee back in shape to play on the team my senior year. This was my last chance. I had to make the team, and I did, but in the practice leading up to our first game, I tore my knee again. I had to sit out my senior year, too."

Kyle Bjornstad didn't play one single second of basketball in high school. He basically had zero chance of making a college team anywhere, much less the storied Oregon State team. It was all over for him.

"I'm not the type of person who succumbs to that," he says. "So Oregon State was off the table. But I had other options. There was a small college in Eugene with a basketball team, and I begged the coach to put me on the practice squad just so I could put on a jersey. Well, he liked me and I started playing pretty well. But deep down in my GUT this wasn't my real goal. I decided to leave and enroll at OSU. I told the assistant coach at my school what I was going to do and he laughed in my face: 'Good luck. Best case is you're going to be a team manager—a ball boy. Enjoy it!'

This just made me more determined. I sent the OSU coach an email explaining my story, got a meeting with him, and got laughed at again. 'See you around,' he said, as he ran me out of his office.

"I refused to give up on my goal. I started hanging around with the players. They didn't have anybody to practice with in the off-season, so I would go and play with them. One day, one of the assistant coaches checked in on us. 'Hey, you're a pretty good player,' he told me, and invited me to join the practice squad, which meant I could fill in at team practices. I did that for a full season. I was not on the team, but it was a start.

"That year, OSU was awful, but I loved it. The team was depressed, and here I was busting my ass on the practice floor, playing with all the hell and vigor I could. The others would say, 'Dude, why are you working so hard? Knock it off.'

"Things got worse. The team went winless that year, 0-18, the worst record in conference history, and the coach was fired mid-season (which never happens); so players started transferring, quitting, and jumping off this Titanic. They were supposed to tour that summer, but their numbers were so low they decided to take me with them. At last I was on the team! I'd get to play three or four minutes, but tried so hard that the team started to love me even though I was such an outlier.

"The new coach was Craig Robinson — Michelle Obama's brother! He started to right the ship, recruiting a new team for the next year, and I steeled myself to be let go. When Coach Robinson called me in, I knew I was going to get cut. It sucks but I get it. I was shocked when he said, 'I've seen you work your butt off. You're a team leader. I'm giving you a full scholarship."

"I couldn't believe it. Here I was—not only a member of the great Oregon State team, but also team captain and on a full-ride scholarship!

"That year our losing streak broke—we went from 0-18 to best turnaround in the league. We even made it to the College Basketball Invitational, a post-season series. After winning one and losing one, we were in the last few seconds of a best-of-three series; we're up only a couple of points, and the coach sends me into the game. 'Coach, what are you doing?' I'm thinking. 'I'm the smallest guy on the team, and you're sending me in now?'

"Fortunately we stay on top and I grab the last rebound just as the buzzer goes off. We had gone from 0-18 the year before to the first post-season tournament OSU had ever won. That night Coach got a phone call from President Obama congratulating him and us on our stunning turnaround."

I love Kyle's story. Sheer GUTs took him from zero chance of ever playing Division I college basketball to being the captain of a team cheered by the President of the United States!

When people look at guys like Kyle, they'd say the odds are against him, but I would say that for a guy who can pull it out of his GUT like that, the odds are always in his favor. Nobody sees and nobody knows what's in the GUT.

Kyle says, "You get that feeling in your GUT that you want something so bad, no matter how long it takes or how bad it hurts, you just go for it. Sometimes you fail—and I can accept failure—but I can't accept looking back and realizing I didn't try." [3]

Kyle Bjornstad *loves* basketball: he's so passionate about it you could also say that basketball *loves him*. He's an ordinary guy, not a big famous celebrity athlete—but a man who lives from the GUT and loves it.

I want you to notice that Kyle is not a celebrity or an Olympian or a genius. But despite Kyle's many setbacks and humiliations, he never, ever lost touch with his passion. The sweat, the hard work, the pain—it all gives him *joy*! I know that doesn't sound reasonable, but it's true. And it's true of everyone who lives from the GUT. It can be true of you!

Sometimes we lose touch with our GUT and get tangled up in a stupid net of petty jealousies or political fights at work or just the everyday aggravations of living. We start to feel sorry for ourselves.

When I go for a run, I typically do a five-mile loop along a biking trail that ends with a steep bridge. One day I was running, and a little girl was coming down the path towards me on a bicycle. She wasn't wearing a helmet. Suddenly, she veered toward a nearby gate, accelerated, and *bam!!!* Hit the gate full force. The impact threw her head over heels onto the pavement.

I ran to help, worried about head trauma. She was beat up, scrapes everywhere, but no broken bones or head injury. Her father, who had been trailing her, came up on his bike as I was caring for her. Gently, I encouraged her to wear a helmet the next time she went for a bike ride. Her father was offended and started screaming profanities at me, telling me to mind my own business.

I shouted back. "I was trying to help your daughter, you ass. If you really cared for her, you wouldn't let her ride a bike without a helmet. It's your fault." Pissed off, I left and started to run again, full of frustration and angrily mumbling to myself.

---

3 Author interview with Kyle Bjornstad, Corvallis, OR, September 12, 2016.

"That stupid dad. How could he criticize me? All I was trying to do was help. He was the irresponsible one. Taking it out on me was pathetic!"

My paced quickened. I just keep on stewing over it, getting angrier by the minute. Before I knew it, I had run the loop faster than I ever had before and was completely exhausted, wiped out. I would never get up that steep bridge staggering like this.

Then far down the path I saw a blurry figure coming toward me, unrecognizable at first, then as I got closer and closer I could see it was a young man in a motorized wheelchair. He had no arms and no legs and was driving his wheelchair with his chin. He looked like he was having the time of his life. He was happy as can be, calling out a cheerful hello as he passed me.

I was amazed. Suddenly I learned a wonderful lesson. You can go through life making a mess, even get in trouble when you're trying your best, and feel sorry for yourself. You can get pissed off all you want, it just makes you tired. But then I think of that young man and realize I have nothing to complain about.

Back home I told my boys about the young man I'd met on the path. "Oh, yes," they said. "That's Gabe Adams and he is awesome. Dad, he's an amazing artist, just using his chin and his iPhone. And he can even dance! He dances with the cheerleaders at basketball games!"

Days later I saw Gabe again, this time at a high school football game where my sons were playing. He left his chair and hopped and bounced up the stadium bleachers without arms and legs and without help to sit with his family. It was a remarkable thing to watch.

Our boys won that night. But a far greater victory is what I witnessed when young Gabe climbed those stairs with a big grin on his face. I have never seen a happier human being. That night I learned that happiness is a choice, and it takes GUTs to make that choice.

Young Gabe Adams loves to dance, and dancing *loves him*. Dancing is in his GUT. Maybe the most inspiring thing I have ever seen is Gabe dancing with the cheerleaders at his high school. He does flips and rolls. He vaults across the room. He springs up and down like a champion gymnast. And he does all of this with no limbs! I call that GUTs.

What are the odds that a young man with no arms or legs could become an accomplished dancer? A million to one against, I guess. Unless that young man has GUTs. Then, believe me, the odds are in his favor.

Over the years I have had the opportunity to coach football at the college, high school and youth league levels. I love coaching, and *coaching loves me*!

My football coaches have been among the greatest blessings in my life. I was very fortunate in my athletic career to have some of the world's finest and brightest coaches—and they taught me more than just football. John Chura, Bill Curry, Ken Blair, and Mac McWhorter all had great influence on me as a young man.

Football has always been important to me. I just love the game, controversies and all. There is something about what it teaches young men that is difficult to put in words. They come to understand the importance of working hard for a goal, doing their part, serving others, and being a leader.

And deep down inside I have always loved to help others, teach others, and coach others. I discovered my love for coaching others when my son Beau was nine and my son Ben was five.

Years ago we moved to Georgia, and my sons wanted to sign up for football, so I took them to their first practices. The coaches were terrible—well-meaning, but just terrible. We were horrified. They screamed at the boys, used disgusting language, berated the kids, and even taught them incorrect and unsafe form. They did not understand the game, nor how to coach so the game was safe and fun.

The Influence of the GUT

Does the GUT influence our feelings and decisions? This question is the subject of many research projects.

An experiment at McMaster University involved two groups of mice, one of them more "timid and docile" than the other, meaning that they were much less likely to take risks. The researchers wiped out the bacteria in the GUTs of both groups of mice, then swapped GUT bacteria and fed each group the bacteria from the other group.

Afterwards, tests showed that the mice had swapped behavior! The normal mice were now the "timid and docile" mice! We are not mice, but is it possible that our GUTs influence our feelings and our thinking much more than we ever suspected?

(Sharon Oosthoek, "GUT Feeling," CBS News, July 14, 2014.)

I found myself going to every practice because I was concerned about my children's safety and wanted to make sure they had a positive experience. So after every practice I would spend countless hours coaching my boys to play with the correct form and giving them positive reinforcement. Before long, a group of concerned parents brought their boys to join my boys for these sessions. Thankfully, we made it through the year without any major incidents.

In the process, I discovered how much I *loved* coaching those kids. Despite my busy schedule, I volunteered the next year to be a head coach, and for the next fifteen years I coached my three boys, Beau, Ben and Jake, until they reached high school. They turned out to be amazing young men and very successful both on the field and in the classroom.

Over those fifteen years, I deepened my understanding of coaching because I wanted to. I even spent some time at Columbia University working through an intensive coaching curriculum, and later helped start an executive coaching practice at FranklinCovey. I discovered that I was built to be a life coach and I love it—it is inside me. I cannot *not* do it.

The funny thing is, I was born to be a coach—not the traditional kind of sports coach, but a life coach. I *love* helping people find their purpose, make the needed course corrections, and succeed in life no matter what the goal.

Today my avocation is my vocation. I believe I can do many other things with excellence, but executive coaching is my sweet spot.

We have our own longings, cravings, and yearnings that come from deep down in the GUT. I get off on coaching people. Kyle Bjornstad couldn't live without basketball. Gabe Adams has dancing in his soul. The woodcutter gets off on splitting wood perfectly. He's no different from diamond cutters who are delighted when a flawless diamond cleaves just right. A pilot who is landing her airliner loves it when she can put the big wheels on the ground so gently that nobody even feels it.

How can you tell work and play apart when you get so much fun and fulfillment from your work? You can't. There's a kind of happiness that comes from doing what your GUT tells you is right for you—and you are even happier when you do it well.

Lots of books will tell you that you should do what you love.

I'm inviting you to do what loves *you*.

You've always known what it is. Although career counselors and placement tests will give you some help, usually they tell you what you already know and what you've always known.

I have a friend who writes. As far back as he can remember, he's been a writer. He wrote TV screenplays when he was six years old. When he was ten he wrote a mystery novel called "The Snail in the Wine Cellar." In junior high he wrote stories about his friends and made money selling them. He wrote an underground newspaper in high school and a novel in college. He has written poems, stories, plays, magazine articles, video scripts, and so many books he's lost count of them all. No matter what job he held, he always ended up writing. Today he makes his living as a writer. Guess what he'll do when he retires?

If you ask him why he writes, he says, "I have to. It owns me. *It's in my GUT.*"

That's my point. My friend never *decided* to be a writer. His GUT decided *for* him. "There's something beautiful about a well-written sentence," he says. "I dream about sentences. I make them up in my head all day. It's sort of like when you love someone. You think about them all the time and you just want to be with them."

My friend would say his *avocation* and his *vocation* are the same.

He's like the poet Robert Frost, whose poem I quoted earlier. Frost had a lot of jobs in his life. He was a farmer, an actor manager, a school teacher. For a while he worked in a power station replacing the burned-out carbon in arc lamps—a dangerous and dirty job that involved hanging from scaffolding fifty feet off the ground.

But he was a poet all the time. It never occurred to him to be or to do anything else, so he wrote poems on the roof of the power station. Regardless of what he did for cash, his real work was poetry. When a poem of his "worked," he would say he had a profound feeling that "something was happening. It was like cutting along a nerve." He loved poetry and he needed poetry— "only when love and need are one is the deed ever really done."

The woodcutter who loves chopping wood might make no sense to you. But to him, not only does chopping wood make sense, *it's the only thing that does.*

Now imagine another guy out there swinging an axe who hates the job. He's exhausted. He hates the sweat, the dirt, the weather, and the pain in his shoulder from overworking it. Wood chips are flying everywhere. He curses the sun for being too hot and the clouds for making it cold. And he counts the minutes until he can quit for the day and do the stuff he *really* loves.

For this guy, chopping wood is *not* play. *Absolutely* not!

But wait. After he gets off, he heads out into the desert in a stock car, speeding around a track, choking on dust and exhaust fumes and sweating and burning up in the sun. It's strenuous. It's dangerous. It takes every muscle and every ounce of skill he has.

But he *loves* it. *And he's not tired at all.*

He's always loved it. As a child he raced cars. As a teenager he couldn't wait to get a car of his own. He knows all about engines and famous stock car drivers and their cars. A race car is more than a hobby for him. He loves it—and *it loves him.*

As far as his wood-chopping job is concerned, *it's just wrong.* In his GUT he knows it's wrong. Does he have to chop wood for a living? Could he make his avocation his vocation? Are there jobs to be had in the world of auto racing and speedways? Where, for him, work can become play?

So what possesses *you*, obsesses *you*, and loves *you*? *What is your GUT telling you?*

Listen. It doesn't matter what anybody else says. It doesn't even matter much what *you* think is the reasonable, practical, sensible, down-to-earth, level-headed thing to do.

Because your GUT doesn't care.

Go With Your GUT!

Answer these questions for yourself. Write down your answers.

1. "If you have GUTs, the odds are always in your favor." What do you think that statement means? Do you believe it's true? Why or why not?

2. Think back as far as you can remember. What did you do when you weren't forced to do something else? What was "play" to you? What did you do as a teenager when you weren't working on school or a job? If you had a whole free day to do what *you* most want to do, how would you spend it?

3. Now check your answers to question 2 against what your GUT is telling you—are you being completely honest about what you hear?

What do you think of your score on the GUTs quiz? What could you do to improve your score? Because the message is unreasonable. Because it's coming from the deepest kind of intuition, the kind we ironically call "counterintuitive."

CHAPTER 2

Why aren't you listening?

Yes, it's counterintuitive to do what other people call dumb things—to stay up late working just because you can't stop, to fly a kite in a storm because you've got to know what lightning is, to create something just because you have to create it or you'll die. It is also very difficult to listen to the deepest parts of your soul with all the constant noise that abounds everywhere.

We don't notice all the noise flying around us. These days most people are surrounded by noise, a lot of noise. The noise from social media, the noise from our smart phones, the noise from games, and the constant pushing of marketing messages from every conceivable source.

Why don't we listen to our GUT?

Here is your GUT telling you what possesses you. It's telling you who you are and what you can be. You find yourself unconsciously pushing the conversation in that direction— toward the thing that obsesses you.

It's what you want to talk about, what you think about, and you can't understand why others can't hear it. It gives you energy and fills your life with excitement.

45

GUTS and Hunches

A hunch is a strong, intuitive feeling that you can't explain. It's one of those GUT feelings.

"I have a hunch that stock is going to go up."

"Why do you think so?"

"I don't know. It's a GUT feeling."

It doesn't really make sense to ask a person "why?" when they have a hunch. It's just a powerful feeling that a certain outcome will take place.

A hunch is different from a guess.

"I guess he's lying" means you're pretty sure. You might have enough facts to draw a reasonable conclusion but not a certain conclusion.

"I have a hunch he's lying" means that something deep down tells you this person is not honest. You might have no facts at all, but your GUT is sending signals that might have no obvious basis at all.

A hunch can become a guess if you get some supporting facts. But a hunch is more like an intuition, a "sixth sense" message.

Are hunches valuable? What do you think?

But not even you . . . *NOT EVEN YOU* . . . are listening.

Why not?

Because you're afraid. That's why you're stuck.

Because of their fears, everyone is stuck one way or another. They don't want to listen to what their GUT is telling them. It requires courage they think they don't have, joy they don't feel, or excitement that frightens them. They'd rather play games, text, surf, watch TV, party, even work—anything to silence that inner voice that challenges them to be what they were meant to be and do what they were meant to do.

We think that what our GUT is telling us is too hard for us. Just look at the odds of success—it's such a long shot. It's too disruptive. We think it's easier to *not* think. We think that the work we do is okay, even though it's not *our* work. And because that work makes us miserable, we think it's even moral, self-sacrificing work. We make ourselves into martyrs, and then we do our best to escape from that work by entertaining ourselves to death on our off hours with sports, nonsense TV, and brainless gaming.

And that's how we shut out that inner voice from deep down that's telling us we're in the wrong place and doing the wrong things.

But here's the thing. That life I just described . . . that's the needlessly *hard* life. It's hard to work on stuff that isn't your work. It's hard to head out every day and do stuff you don't care about. It's hardest of all to realize that in those hours when you think you're having fun you're just fooling yourself—you're in escape mode because you can't face what your GUT is telling you.

Here's why your life is hard:

- *Stuck mindset.* Your mind is stuck. You ignore your GUT that's telling you to change. You're in a place people call the "comfort zone," and it's a deadly place. It's like quicksand—the more you struggle inside of it, the more it pulls you down.

- *Overwhelm.* You're way under water with dumb things at work, social media updates, your blinking, buzzing phone, the endless distractions that shut out that inner voice begging you to STOP and LISTEN (and you're sort of relieved that they do). You consistently consider too many things and freeze or do nothing.

- *Efficiency.* In one motion you get up and shower and drink something and get online and work and work and eat something and work and come home and flop down and get back online and fall asleep—it's just one uninterrupted stream of habits that take no thought at all. You "rinse and repeat" daily because it's better than being afraid.

- *Loneliness.* You feel alone, and virtually no one sees your potential or supports your efforts to go after your dreams. Often feelings of loneliness can lead to self-medication and other destructive behaviors. So you try very hard not to think about it.

- *Sheer fear.* It's built into us. Ages ago, the people who successfully escaped from tigers and snakes and wolves became our ancestors. The ones who didn't make it did not. So we descend from generations upon generations of people who could run faster than the next person—otherwise we would not be here. So it's normal to be scared of big GUTsy things like changing our lives.

"I think it's good that I get scared because, if you never get scared, you don't have any need for GUTs."

-Tracy Morgan, actor and comedian

So why is your life hard? Because even if you do start listening to that inner voice and making that big change, *you could fail.*

Failure.

It's the biggest fear of all. I don't believe that our lack of talent or money or looks or our crummy circumstances or our family pressures or anything outside ourselves can cause us to fail. I believe way deep down that our greatest fear is that we will fail *ourselves.* We believe the odds are against us. We believe that we can't do it. That we don't have what it takes to achieve our dreams. That we haven't got the GUTS!

Yes, even thinking about it is scary.

But, as everyone knows, scary can be fun and exciting.

Crouch at the top of the ski hill. Sit at the top of the roller coaster. Step off the platform and go bungee-jumping. Pick up your phone to call someone for a date. Stand up to give a speech. Come off the bench and get in the game. Wake up on your wedding day.

What do you feel in your GUT?

You know how it feels. It's like when you're moving along smoothly and all of a sudden the car or the plane hits a bump.

You go airborne for a second. That feeling in your GUT can be scary but also exhilarating.

It's called a "thrill."

It's a sinking feeling that both excites and terrifies. You might lose your lunch, but you might also have the best time of your life.

Technically, your adrenal glands are pumping out a soup of stress-related hormones that make you feel anxious. But the beauty of it is, they make you feel energized at the same time— inspired, lifted, and alive!

What are the odds of success in life for a kid who was drinking and using drugs and being abused before he was ten? Pretty lousy?

Growing up in Las Vegas on the fringes of the mob and motorcycle gangs, I suffered all manner of abuse as a child. I was brutally beaten, set on fire, and used as a human dart board; I started using drugs and alcohol at age eight, and was abused in every way imaginable. Those who were responsible for caring for me, although trying to do good, failed miserably and did not provide a healthy, stable home life. This environment had a huge negative impact on my self-worth.

Fortunately for me, my escape was running and football. As a kid I ran all the time: it just felt good. I would run to the store, my friend's house, school—just everywhere. It felt so good to run and I got good at it. Football was another story. I learned early that I could take some of life's frustrations out on the field and knock the crap out of people and I was praised. So I naturally excelled at football. In school I was in "special ed.," barely passing from one grade to the next.

When I was in junior high school, I joined the track team. I was the best on our team at the 440, 880, shot put, and discus. It was strange to see a kid 13 years old and six-foot-two and 190 pounds be successful at running, but most people expected me to throw implements far. I started getting some positive reinforcement for my achievements, and it made me feel proud.

| GUTS

One day after track practice, my older stepbrother picked me up and took me to an abandoned construction site. There he exposed me to all manner of drugs. I got really sick and should have been hospitalized but didn't want anyone to know what was going on. A few days later I went to track practice, stretched, and started to run a warm-up lap around a dirt track where we practiced. About half way around that track I experienced extreme pain in my chest and could not breathe and collapsed in the dirt.

On my hands and knees heaving for breath, I had an incredible epiphany. If I kept doing what my family was doing I was going to end up like them. Something deep in my soul rejected that notion—*"not like them,"* it said. "They are miserable, and you do not have to be like them. You, my friend, have a choice to become someone special."

Crawling there in the dirt, sick and anxious and nauseated, I could hear a voice inside.

It was telling me that this was not the way my life should be. It was telling me not to be afraid any longer. It was telling me to get up and be true to who I really was.

So I got up and slapped the dust off, and I started a new life. And I haven't looked back since.

That day a bold vision sprang into my mind. It was so strong it gave me meaning and purpose. It fueled my fire and immediately changed my trajectory. The very next day I started doing things differently. I stopped doing drugs and drinking alcohol and started down the path to achieve my wildest dreams. From that day until now I have spent most days getting up early and going to bed late, working tirelessly on living my hopes and dreams. It has taken GUTs to do such a thing. It has not always been easy, but I have been happy through it all. That day was the defining day in my life.

Was everything smooth after that? Did I fail and fail and flop on my face again and again?

No, yes, yes, and yes.

But I always hear that voice deep down telling me not to be afraid, to get up and start again. The place where your dreams are is on the other side of fear. And every time I get up, the odds change in my favor.

Now here's the great secret:

Perfect love casts out fear.

This whole book is about love. It's about loving who you really are and doing what you really love. It's about loving the people who love you and lift you and who you lift in return. It's about loving your *life.*

Your GUT is unhappy if you settle for anything less than a life of love.

- Love sees the good in the world and in people.

- The more you love, the greater your propensity to love.

- Love breaks down barriers.

- Love opens hearts and minds.

- Love increases hope and belief in the future

- Love sacrifices for others.

I believe love is a GUT instinct.

For instance, on a cold January morning in New York City, Wesley Autrey was waiting for the train at the 137th Street subway stop with his two young daughters. Suddenly, a young man standing by him suffered a seizure and spiraled down onto the tracks. *Without hesitating*, Wesley jumped from the platform to pull the man to safety. But the train was coming too fast.

Disoriented, the young man tried to escape. Wesley yanked him into a narrow, muddy trench between the rails just as the train hurtled over their bodies. The space between Wesley's head and the subway cars was the length of a credit card, but by crouching down hard he saved both himself and the young man.

"Am I dead?" the man asked, as the train screeched to a stop.

"No, we're under the train," Wesley said. "You feel me pinching you? We're very much alive."

When Wesley got back on the platform, there was no trace of his ordeal except for a grease stain on the back of his powder-blue ski cap.

Soon known as the "Subway Superman," Wesley became famous for his heroism. He was invited to the White House, recognized at the Super Bowl, and interviewed on NBC's Tonight Show[4].

Why would Wesley Autrey, an ordinary construction worker (and a dad with two little girls) leap in front of an oncoming subway train to save a complete stranger? I don't have an answer, but Wesley said he heard a voice that said, "I can do this." [5] I like to think it was what we call a GUT reaction, an instinctive impulse to do the right thing—and what is more "right" than to save a fellow human being from disaster? Isn't that what we call love?

The Bible says, "Greater love hath no man than this, that he lay down his life for his friends."

A few years ago, a young woman named Lora Shrake was driving one day through the farm country of Illinois when she saw something horrendous going on in a paddock by the road: a massive bull was attacking a woman, goring her with its horns and tossing her in the air.

---

4 McShane, Larry, "Subway Hero Wesley Autrey Has Holiday Reunion with the Man He Saved," New York Daily News, January 4, 2009. http://www.nydailynews.com/news/subway-hero-wesley-autrey-holiday-reunion-man-saved-article-1.420219

5 Brice, Makini,"The Psychology of Altruism," Medical Daily, August 10, 2012. http://www.medicaldaily.com/psychology-altruism-saving-others-lives-inherently-selfish-act-241890

Lora stopped her car and rushed to the woman's aid. Between her and the woman was a serious electric fence. Lora didn't flinch—she took a jolt of high voltage when she wriggled through the fence, but charged right ahead. Seeing a length of rubber tubing on the ground, she grabbed it and started smacking the angry bull on the nose with it, just hard enough to distract the animal so the injured woman could crawl through the fence. Lora escaped too, thank goodness.

Why would Lora Shrake, an ordinary Illinois college kid, take such an amazing risk on behalf of someone she had never seen or heard of before? Why was she so willing to lay down her life for a stranger?

When asked, she replied, "I didn't really take the moment to think of what might happen." [6]

It was a *GUT decision!*

"Courage, sacrifice, determination, commitment, toughness, heart, talent, GUTs. That's what little girls are made of."

-Bethany Hamilton, professional surfer
and shark-attack survivor

Everybody would agree that Wesley Autrey and Lora Shrake have GUTs. It took GUTs to do what they did, but it also took *character* to do what they did. I want to connect the idea of GUTs with the idea of character. I think GUTs means more than crazy daring or audacity or machismo or bravado. I think it means a *lot* more than that. What really takes GUTs is the bravest thing of all: to truly love others.

Wesley Autrey and Lora Shrake had that greater love. And perfect love casts out fear.

---

6 "Hometown Hero," Indianapolis Star, May 4, 1996, 30; Brice, op. cit.

| GUTS

Tell me what you love and I'll tell you about your character—the kind of person you are.

Is it possible that GUTs and character are the same thing? I believe so.

When you really start to listen to that deep inner voice, when you find what you really love, you'll find that love is greater than fear. In the words of the poet Shel Silverstein,

There is a voice inside of you

That whispers all day long

"I feel this is right for me,

I know that this is wrong."

No teacher, preacher, parent, friend

Or wise man can decide

What's right for you—just listen to

The voice that speaks inside.[7]

---

7 Silverstein, Shel, "The Voice," Where the Sidewalk Ends, Harper-Collins, 2014

Go With Your GUT!

Answer these questions for yourself. Write down your answers.

1. Have you ever loved doing something that also made you fearful—like sports or playing music for other people? How did you get past your fears?

2. When in your life have you been most excited? Write about that experience and why it was so thrilling for you.

3. In what ways are you "stuck"? What one or two things could you start doing right now to free yourself?

CHAPTER 3

Why are you trying to avoid it?

Because you think you've got to show "grit"—you've got to show you can stand it— you tolerate a boring life of tedious meetings, dreary commutes, mind-numbing projects, tiresome people—uninspiring, repetitive, useless tasks that sap the life out of you. "Grit" is slowly killing you.

"It's too late for me. I'm too invested in my job, my boss's priorities, and my crappy life to make any serious changes. Wouldn't I be copping out if I changed? Shouldn't I have the grit to grind on through?"

Even if we hear that deep-down voice telling us what we *should* do with our lives, we still think it's too late for us, we're in too far, and we can't turn back. We've got responsibilities, we've made commitments. We have to "stick it out, go all the way, hang in there, go the limit, hold on, tough it out, and 'perseverate.'"

Even if it kills us.

"Grit" Can Work Against You

In the acclaimed film Bridge Over the River Kwai, Colonel Nicholson is a British officer in a Japanese prisoner-of-war camp. To show what British soldiers are capable of doing, and to demonstrate "grit," he volunteers his battalion to build a railroad bridge for the enemy.

Laboring through mud, disease, and tropical heat, Nicholson and his men at last create a sturdy, well-made bridge "to stand for 600 years!" as he boasts.

Only at the very end does Nicholson realize to his horror that his gritty achievement is helping the enemies of his country, and he destroys it.

Not everything is worth doing, let alone persisting at it.

Not everyone who works hard is doing something that should be done.

People with "grit" often succeed when it would have been better to do something else. It might be "a costly or inefficient success that could have been easily surpassed by alternative courses of action."

"Grit" can often work against you.

"Gritty people sometimes exhibit what psychologists call 'nonproductive resistance.' They try, try again . . . driven by a desperate (and anxiety-provoking) need to prove their competence."

Alfie Kohn, "Sometimes It's Better to Quit," Washington Post, April 4, 2014.

"It takes GUTs to get out of the ruts."

-Robert H. Schuller

Everybody talks about "grit" these days. Grit is sand, dust, gravel, or pebbles that get into a machine and wear it out. It can also mean toughing it out, as in "He gritted his teeth and knocked the other guy out." It can also mean "courage or resolve."

We talk about great athletes with "grit." Great performers who beat impossible odds because of their "grit." We praise soldiers, CEOs, and salespeople with "grit."

But how is that some people show a lot of grit but get nowhere? They grind away forever but make no progress at all. And I'm wondering if that doesn't describe most people—conscientious, hard-working people, certainly—but also unhappy and unfulfilled people.

In her famous study of grit, Angela Duckworth tells a story about the winners of a national spelling contest—about their intense practice sessions, years of preparation, and demonstrations of "grit." She notes "grittier spellers practiced more than less gritty spellers." [8]

8 Duckworth, Angela, Grit: The Power of Passion and Perseverance, Scribner, 2016, 124.

But isn't this the same as saying, "spellers who practice more practice more than spellers who practice less"?

I have a friend who has what is called an "eidetic memory" for words. He can spell every word you can throw at him—it doesn't matter what word it is—long or short, simple or complicated. Something in his brain makes it possible for him to spell anything in the English language *error-free* whether he has ever seen the word or not. He has easily won every spelling contest he ever entered. He could win in his sleep. He simply cannot miss.

What would endless practice do for him? Should he show some "grit" and memorize the whole dictionary?

Should he spend endless hours mastering the complicated rules of English spelling with their thousands of exceptions?

He doesn't need to. It's "just there." In his brain, in his GUT.

So what is "just there" inside you?

Of course, you can get better at spelling if you practice. You can generally get better at anything if you practice long and hard enough, and if you really want to, you should. But it doesn't mean that thing is in your GUT.

In the city where I live they hold a world-class piano competition for young players. They come from all over the world—Russia, Europe, Korea, everywhere. It's fascinating to watch the final night of the competition when the top three contestants play unbelievably tough piano works with a full orchestra and audience. You can feel the tension in the hall as they compete for first prize.

All the players are great. Technically strong, highly disciplined, and well prepared. But by the end of the night, everybody—I mean *everybody*—knows who won.

It's the pianist with GUTs. The one who overwhelms you with joy, the one who makes real music because it comes from somewhere most of us can't even define—from way, way down inside.

Every one of the contestants has worked incredibly hard, but on most of them you see the face of pain. You see a mighty tide of stress. You hear it in their playing. You feel it in the way they hold their bodies back. These are the ones who have "grit."

But they don't have music in the GUT.

The same is true in athletics.

Nobody works harder than the terrific NBA guard Stephen Curry. Some people call him the best basketball player in the world.

When Steph first came to Kobe Bryant's basketball camp as a 16-year-old, the coaches saw something strange in him. The top young shooters in the country were there. Nearly all of them were headed for the NBA, and they all had "grit." But Steph stood out.

Coach Alan Stein remembers, "The least recognized player there was Stephen Curry, but I knew immediately that he was the most impressive and would be a future NBA superstar. Here's how I knew that: It was all because of his work habits. By the time workout started . . . Steph had already made 150 shots in a full sweat. And after workout, he wouldn't leave the court until he'd swished five free-throws in a row. You know how hard that is?" [9]

Yes, Steph is a hard worker, and he's had to overcome all kinds of obstacles to become a superstar—he was considered undersized, he had ankle injuries. Perseverance is one thing, but as sportswriter Zito Madu said in 2015, "It's entirely another to become *Steph,* the outrageous thrilling shooter and playmaker for the NBA's best team." He's not the crazy monster that most NBA players are. He looks like an ordinary guy, but there's something inside of him that goes beyond hard work.

Madu nails it: "Hard work will always be the Robin to the Batman of natural talent. Even those who preach the miracles of staying later

9 "This Trainer Knew Then-16-Year-Old Steph Curry Would be a Future NBA Superstar: The Reason Why Is So Motivating," ViralHoops.com, n.d. http://www.viralhoops.com/stephen-curry-motivational-video/

than your competition" have to admit that what's inside matters more. As for Steph, he was "clearly otherworldly" at an early age.[10]

Of course Steph works hard, but nothing can take the place of what's deep down inside. So what's down inside of you? What is extraordinary in ordinary old you?

Supposedly, "grit" is a moral virtue. Watching a tennis match on TV, I once heard an English color commentator expressing doubt about a certain player: "I don't think he has the sand to win." Puzzled, I found out later that in Britain "to have sand" means to be willing to "grit your teeth and muddle through." We admire people who have "sand." We have a high regard for people with boldness, determination, and perseverance. And why not?

Well, maybe we shouldn't. It all depends on the ends they have in mind. Some people in history have pursued some awful goals with determination and perseverance. In the ancient Greek myth of Sisyphus, a man who offended the gods was doomed to roll a giant boulder up a mountain, only to watch it roll back down to the bottom—and to repeat this useless task for eternity. No question Sisyphus showed "grit." He worked really hard, no doubt grunting and sweating and toiling at it for a very long time, but to what end?

We all know about tasks that are called "Sisyphean." Like washing the car just before it rains or picking up the baby's toys—you're doomed to do it all over again pretty soon.

But spending your life in a Sisyphean career just because you feel like you ought to show "grit"? What kind of a life is that? What if it's all pain, depression, and futility? America is number one in the world in a lot of things—one of them is the number of people who hate their jobs. More than half! [11]

---

10 Madu, Zito, "Stephen Curry Shows Normal People What True Mastery Is," SBNation, March 12, 2015. http://www.sbnation.com/2015/3/12/8173873/stephen-curry-highlights-golden-state-warriors-mastery

11 Brownstone, Sydney, "Everyone in the World Hates Their Jobs—But Americans Hate Theirs the Most," FastCompany, November 18, 2013.

Why is that? Why are so many of us working so hard at rolling the boulder up the hill? Could it be that we feel it's "the right thing to do"? What kind of virtue is that?

In the film *The Shawshank Redemption*, an inmate named Andy has been unjustly imprisoned. He seems to be living the kind of Sisyphean life that the other inmates live, as so many of us who are "caged up" do every day. But he isn't. He has a drive in his GUT to be free and to live by the Pacific Ocean, which is sort of a symbol of the great life. So every day he digs a little deeper at the drain in his cell. The odds are a million to one that he will ever dig through. He does this for twenty years, but in the end escapes through half a mile of sewer pipe.

Back in the prison, his friend Red had resigned himself to the Sisyphean life. It was all "grit," all enduring, just pushing on hopelessly every day: "Same old shit, different day," he would say each morning. But Andy's hopefulness was contagious, and Red began to feel a stirring deep down inside. When Andy finally escaped, Red found that thrill overwhelming:

I find I'm so excited that I can barely sit still or hold a thought in my head. I think it's the excitement only a free man can feel. A free man at a start of a long journey whose conclusion is uncertain. I hope I can make it across the border. I hope to see my friend and shake his hand. I hope the Pacific is as blue as it has been in my dreams. I hope.

What kind of cage are you in? What is your "blue Pacific Ocean"? Can you make it across the border? Of course you can.

There are lots of people who work like mad but love it. They feel pain just like anyone else, they crawl through the muck too, they struggle and sacrifice—but they delight in all of it.

Years ago while attending Georgia Tech, my favorite professor was Dr. Philip Adler. He was my "Andy."

Dr. Adler was notoriously talented at creating a high-intensity atmosphere in the classroom. He was a strong Socratic teacher and required us to memorize everything that we covered in class before the next class. He had a photographic memory and knew everyone's name the first day of class. He expected and demanded unbelievable performance from his students. To this day, when I visit with him he fully expects me to be able to teach him at a moment's notice what he taught me so many years ago. The funny thing is that I remember everything he taught me with ease.

I've often wondered why Dr. Adler had such an impact on me when other teachers didn't even register. You know how one or two teachers stand out in your memory so tall that the others seem to disappear by comparison? For me, that was Dr. Adler. Teaching was in his *GUT*. It's what he lived for.

He taught me that learning was exciting—hard, but sensationally fun. He stimulated me every minute. As a student, I came out of the kind of spiritual and mental cage that Red inhabited in *Shawshank* and found my "blue Pacific Ocean." Dr. Adler also taught me that escaping the mentality of a Red was tough.

It was Dr. Adler who asked this most profound question: Why do human beings resist change?

Because, he used to say, they think they need to conserve energy. They assume that the more energy they conserve, the easier their life will be, and that maybe they will even live longer.

The exact opposite is true. People are not batteries: they don't "die" from using energy. I know this is counterintuitive, but actually the more people try to conserve their energy by getting into habits or routines that make life easier and avoiding meaningful, creative work, the sooner they lose their ability to think creatively or actively meet new situations over time. As soon as there is a major shift in the environment or economy, they collapse. When a few years ago 30 million people lost their jobs, more than half stayed out of the workforce permanently.

Why? My theory is that they had allowed themselves to slowly die—doing the same old things forever ("conserving energy").

When their environment drastically changed, they were not ready for it. They had lost the will. They had burned out on "grit" for too long. They had "no GUTs."

"I guess it comes down to a simple choice, really. Get busy living or get busy dying."

– The Shawshank Redemption

Living a life ignoring your innate purpose and meaning is just grinding through your days, getting lost on your journey. You spend your days working hard, giving effort, but for what? Why? To pay your bills? To eke out some extra money to indulge in trendy pleasures? Or because you feel like you "have to"—you've gotta show "grit."

I think "grit" limits people. I agree with one smart observer's question about "grit": "Is there any good football team that *doesn't* believe in endless practice, endurance, overcoming pain and exhaustion? All professional teams train hard, so grit can't be the necessary explanation for . . . success." [12]

Have you ever worked your butt off – done well, accomplished the goal – but you just felt exhausted and frustrated with the energy it took to finish the project or finally achieve the goal? We know that millions of people work hard every day and still feel empty. Most people work in jobs they don't like and do the minimum work required to stay employed. They can't give their best at work because most of the time their job doesn't align with the GUT.

The result is pain—and not just in the GUT.

In the next chapter, we'll find out how to get past "grit" and find answers in the GUT.

---

12 Denby, David, "The Limits of Grit," The New Yorker, June 21, 2016.

Go With Your GUT!

Answer these questions for yourself. Write down your answers.

1.   What is the difference between "grit" and "GUTs"? Between grinding through the daily rut and working hard at what matters most to you—loving the sacrifice it takes?   Do you feel like you have "grit"? Is it working for or against you?

2.   Have you ever worked your butt off—done well, accomplished the goal—but you just feel exhausted? When you were frustrated with the energy it took to finish the project or finally achieve the goal?

3.   Have you ever wondered, "Where did my energy go? Why do I feel like I am slowly dying and my life just doesn't mean that much?" Do you feel life your life is being sucked out the window of the office at work?

CHAPTER 4

Do you have the GUTs to change?

You don't need grit. What you really need is GUTs—the fortitude to take that spark of inspiration and to fan it into a flame. What will be your life's great contribution? And do you have the GUTs to make it happen? Your "Big Why" or purpose is the ultimate renewable energy source.

Okay, so you're in pain because you *just can't change*, right?

You'd rather take the pain of a purpose-starved life than go deep and find the fire at your own center?

Or would you rather go for it?

To see if you have the GUTs for change, let's understand what gets in the way of change. In his book *Change or Die*, Dr. Alan Deutschman says most of us resist change big time. Even when faced with death if we don't change, only one in nine of us will actually change our lives. Doctors say to us:

- If you don't lose some weight you will die

- If don't stop drinking or doing drugs you will die

- If you don't get some exercise you will die

- If you don't cut down on the stress you will die

- But we won't, so we die.

If you look at people who have had open-heart surgery to save their lives, 90 percent of them never change the very habits that made surgery necessary in the first place. [13] So they die anyway.

Over the past twenty years, I have studied change. The topic is fascinating to me. I have made significant changes myself along the way, so I know it is possible to change in big ways. Here are the four things that I believe get in the way of change:

- Stinking Thinking (You mean I can't succeed the way I am now?)

- Lack of Purpose (What difference can I make?)

- Lack of Love (Who cares if I change or not?)

- Lack of a Process (How do you change anyway?)

Let's drill down on each of these barriers to change.

Stinking Thinking

A good many of us just stink at thinking. We are blind to our blindness. We just expect that it will work out for us. "Okay, so I don't exercise or eat right—I won't get heart disease! Not me! That's for all those other poor human beings. The laws of physics don't apply to me."

Or we'd rather just not think about it. We get overwhelmed with the idea of change, so we freeze and do nothing. I have an acquaintance, a man who won't go to the doctor because, he

---

13 Deutschman, Alan, Change or Die: The Three Keys to Change at Work or Life, HarperBusiness, 2007, 1-2, 4.

says, "I just don't think about it." His children are in trouble with drugs but he does nothing about it. I don't think he's in denial—I think he just doesn't think very much about anything.

Or we continue to do the same things over and over again, expecting things will change on their own. We'll be fit and healthy and wealthy one of these days. We'll have a great family someday. "It's going to work out great! Just don't ask me how."

With this kind of thinking, how will you ever discover your great contribution—or make it, for that matter? So ask yourself, does your thinking stink?

Lack of Purpose

Another big obstacle to change is the lack of a "why." Why change?

Because we don't have an ultimate end in mind for our lives. We live in a fog. We live in our primal, reptilian brain state, seeking only to satisfy our basic needs to survive and be safe and be entertained. But we are far more than our basic needs—we are human beings driven by high purpose. We can actually get sick if we don't pursue that purpose.

I Knew Deep Down

Many moons ago I fell very hard for a man who was very wrong for me. I was infatuated with him immediately and the symphony of warning bells was drowned out by an inundation of emotions I had never felt before.

Deep down, I knew something was off. I knew I couldn't trust him and I knew the relationship would end in disaster. I didn't want to admit it though, and planted my feet firmly in denial-ville. I never felt that way about anyone before and the prospect of him not being on the same page was too painful a pill to swallow....so I didn't.

In time, my instincts gave me a big "I told you so." Everything I suspected turned out to be true and the most painful probably in the history of the world (or at least, in the history of my life) followed.

Looking back, it's frustrating to think how much time, energy, and hurt I would have spared myself had I listened to my instincts.

-Sabrina Alexis, lifestyle writer for A New Mode.com

Sabrina Alexis, "The Importance of Trusting Your GUT," A New Mode.com, n.d.

Creating your own bold purpose in life doesn't come free. It requires you to use your higher brain function.

The scholar Jonathan Haidt likens the brain to an elephant with a little driver sitting on top. The elephant is the giant part of the brain that does everything automatically—breathing, pumping blood, putting you to sleep and waking you up, telling you you're hungry, tying your shoes—all the habitual stuff you do without thinking much or at all about it.

But the little driver is in charge of where the elephant goes. The driver is the higher brain function. If the driver is skillful and has a clear destination, the elephant will go where the driver tells it to go. On the other hand, if the driver has no idea where to go, the elephant will just make its own way. It will go where it wants to go, and who knows where it will end up? [14]

You're the driver. You decide on the destination. No one can make that decision for you. Others might influence it, but the choice is yours. You might think things like "I never had a chance" or "I was born this way" or "it's too hard," but don't fool yourself into thinking someone or something other than yourself ever chooses your purpose in life. *You* do it.

It's true that the elephant has a mind of its own. It has wants and desires and appetites that are different from the driver's. It doesn't like hard going or heavy lifting any more than you do. Driving an elephant is not easy. But remember—*you* are the driver, not the elephant.

So where do you find your life's purpose—your end in mind, your exciting reason for living, your passion, your legacy, your contribution?

Again, no one can tell you what that is. You are the discoverer of that purpose—no one else can do it, or should do it.

Please remember that most of us settle for something less than "purpose." We settle for goals, aims, targets, objectives. Don't

---

14 Haidt, Jonathan, The Happiness Hypothesis, Basic Books, 2006, xi.

get me wrong—there's nothing bad about those. But let's be careful. Suppose I decide I want to learn to play the guitar. It's a goal. It's an objective. But it is not a *life purpose*. It might be a means to an end, but it is not an end in itself.

Finding your life purpose is tougher than deciding on a goal, like learning to cook or climbing a mountain or winning the Super Bowl or taking every single one of the Viking Cruises.

As the great scientist Daniel Kahneman has said, "When faced with a difficult question, we often answer an easier one instead, usually without noticing the substitution." [15]The easier question is "what are my goals?" The difficult question is "why?"

To get the answer to "why" you have to go into your GUT.

"I was one who seeks and still am," said Demian in Hermann Hesse's famous book, "but I no longer seek in the stars or in books; I'm beginning to hear the teachings of my blood within me." [16]

You won't find the answer to "why" in anything external—"stars or books" or anything else. You'll find it internally, in the deepest part of yourself. It's in the blood, it's in the GUT, it's as much a part of you as your face or your hands. It's the "fire in the belly" that you've heard about.

This kind of fire in the belly doesn't come from eating chili peppers; it's an intense internal drive that is unique to you, that consumes you if you don't express it.

It has been said of Ludwig Van Beethoven that he had it—boundless "fire in the belly" [17] that drove him to create some of the greatest music in history. He played music "with irresistible fire and mighty force." People who knew him worried about the "chronic pain in the GUT" that he suffered from but which also seemed part of what moved him forward. He was never quite

---

15 Kahneman, Daniel, Thinking Fast and Slow, Farrar, Strauss & Giroux, 2013, 12.

16 Hesse, Hermann, Demian: The Story of Emil Sinclair's Youth, Simon & Schuster, 2015,

17 Swafford, Jan, Beethoven: Anguish and Triumph, 79, 410.

satisfied but exhilarated and thrilled by the chance to make his own grand music.

Which he couldn't hear! He was deaf.

What are the odds that a deaf man could become the world's greatest composer of music?

Even though he couldn't hear a note of music, when the fire was in him, the odds turned in his favor.

Beethoven was a genius, but "fire in the belly" is not reserved for geniuses. Everybody has it. You have it. It might be a low fire because you've deprived it of the space and the fuel it needs to flame up. And you might have to dig to find it. But there is a process, a pilgrimage I call it, to get to a clear understanding of the personal passion you were born with.

The journey to discover your purpose can be tough because it requires incredible honesty on your part and a lot of deep introspection. What will you be known for? What will your life's great contributions be? I call the answers to these questions the *Big Why*. The Big Why can be hard to wrap your head around.

Lack of Love

The next obstacle to change is a lack of love.

Maybe we don't love others enough to want to contribute to their lives. Maybe they don't love us. Maybe we don't love ourselves enough to make the effort to find and live out our own great purpose in life.

Human beings crave connection. A few people who loved me for no good reason and reached up, out, and across social barriers to me changed my trajectory. I would be dead, insane, or in prison without them. Because they loved me, I loved them and I grew to feel *accountable* to them. They are part of my Big Why—I owe them and would never want to let them down. Their love and support of me over all these years is immeasurable. I can never pay them back for what they did for me and taught me. But what I can do is bring them honor—to help others and live my life to the best of my ability.

Few people have never felt rejected. Most of us have experienced it. What does it feel like? *A punch in the GUT*. We undergo actual pain, sometimes to the point of sickness. (Doctors now tell us that the neural pathways involved in romantic rejection and stomach pain actually overlap.)[18]

We should listen to our GUT. It's telling us that the answer to our pain is not found in having others love us. It's found in loving *them*. Love is the single most powerful force on the earth. The key here is to serve and love others *without expectation.* The key is not to try to deserve their love, but to hold yourself accountable for giving what you have to give.

In life, we all fall short of perfection. We all make mistakes. We all fail to live up to others' expectations of us, and they fail to live up to ours. Love and forgiveness fixes all of that. Love is the greatest igniter of change.

"If you have the GUTs to keep making mistakes, your wisdom and intelligence leap forward with huge momentum."

-Holly Near, singer and actress

To actively, generously show your love to others—to contribute to their happiness—makes you happy, too, and that's not just a feel-good myth. It's an actual feel-good effect in the brain. Scientists call it "giver's glow" and it's "triggered by brain chemistry." There are several different happiness chemicals that flood the brain when we give loving service to others, "including dopamine,

---

18 Park, Alice, "Why the Pain of Romantic Rejection Feels Like a Punch in the GUT," Time, March 28, 2011.

endorphins that give people a sense of euphoria, and oxytocin, which is associated with tranquility, serenity, or inner peace." [19]

Lack of a Change Process

I said that change is a process, a pilgrimage to find the Big Why. Without that process, that new behavior, you will probably not find what you're looking for. There are four steps.

1. Face the Facts. First, you need to face up to the fact that you have been leading a safe life instead of an exciting life. You have been paying a high price for security, and that price is having to live out a charade of a life every day. You need to face the fact that it will take as much energy to create the life you're really meant for as to create the false life you've been leading. It might even take *more* energy—but it will be infinitely more satisfying and thrilling for you. So you need to put the past behind you instead of in front of you.

2. Understand Your Big Why. Second, you need to understand that inner fire. What is the "yes" burning inside of you, as Stephen R. Covey used to say? What exactly is your Big Why? You can't know this unless you explore your own inner self—what we are calling "listening to your GUT."

You've got to give it space. Take a shower, go for a walk or a bike ride, sleep on it. Let your mind wander. Take a notebook and a pencil and sit under a tree. Ask yourself these questions:

- "What kind of person am I really?"

- "What have I always wanted to be?"

- "What do I love?"

- "What excites me more than anything?"

- "When has my heart ever been really into something?"

19 Renter, Elizabeth, "What Generosity Does to Your Brain and Life Expectancy," US News & World Report, May 1, 2015.

- "What would I do all day long if I were free to do it?" (Seriously!)

- "What should my contribution be—to my loved ones, to the world?"

- "What do I want people to say about me when I'm gone?"

Really think about these questions. It might be helpful to write down your thoughts about each one.

Now write down your Big Why—the answer to the Big Question: "What do I want to do with my life?" Make it a page or a paragraph or just a sentence—or even a single word—but here's a caution: Don't make a list. Too many people make a "bucket list" of stuff they want to do before they kick the bucket and then call that their "life purpose." That isn't a life purpose—that's a grab bag of adventures.

There's nothing wrong with a bucket list, and a bucket list might help you decide what your life's purpose is. But the Big Why is bigger than any list of activities. It's beneath the list. It underlies and surrounds the list. It's the foundation of the list.

3. Check Your GUT Feelings. Third, once you have at least the beginning of an answer, check it against your GUT feelings. Label your feelings: "excited, nervous, scared, thrilled, ready!" Professor Melody Wilding of Hunter College says, "Do a body scan of what's going on for you. You may think, I feel nervous right now, or I feel like I'm not sure what's coming next. Use those skills of emotional labeling to get in touch with what your GUT might be saying to you." [20]
 When you reach the point of excitement—the point at which you can't wait to start—you'll know you've found your Big Why!

---

20 Funk, Liz, 'The Hidden Power in Trusting Your GUT Instincts," Fast Company, April 7, 2016.

4. Give It Time. Typically, change takes time. That fire in your belly can burn out really fast if you put too much pressure on it. You need to keep it burning at a steady rate.

If you like goals, set goals that fit your Big Why. Typically, a goal is the "Big What" because of the Big Why. The Big Why is the perpetual fuel that keeps hope alive and helps you move forward. Make your goals small, particularly at first. Don't make too many of them—one or two at a time. Then check your progress every week at least. Please don't expect big progress. Those small steps add up to big changes in the long run.

New behaviors require constant course corrections. You'll wander off course sometimes. Just remember that when you drive a car or pilot a plane, you're constantly making little course corrections. The driver of a car usually isn't even aware of those corrections, but that's what the big wheel in front of the driver is for.

Think about the people who make dumb goals—"I'm going to lose 50 pounds in ten minutes" type goals—and fall on their faces every time. Maybe you're one of those people who have suffered through unrealistic goals only to fail in the end.

Those "overnight-fix" goals don't work for most of us. People who make them kind of deserve to fail.

But once you're into the Big Why, you're up to your neck in excitement. You don't need the ambitious goals. You'd be doing this anyway because it's your thing. It might be hard going—physically or mentally—but you're totally *there*, you're absorbed, you're focused like never before. You don't run out of fuel because your work renews you constantly. Your Big Why is your ultimate "renewable energy source"!

Why is that so? Because you *love what you're doing*!

The outcome is important, but in a way it's not the point. You just enjoy being a pilgrim on your own path, and you enjoy it so much you almost don't notice that the work is hard and the path is long.

So that's the process for finding your Big Why.

Once you find it, it'll totally transform your life.

"Some people aim at nothing in life and hit it with amazing accuracy."

–Aman Jassal, author

Let me tell you about my mother, my closest and best example of a person who found her purpose. Once she did, she made more changes to her life than anyone I have ever seen. Growing up, I lived in a crazy family, as I've told you. My mom made a lot of mistakes that led to a lot of suffering in my early years.

But I remember just loving her, for no good reason, I guess— forgiving her for all the chaos and craziness. She had a lot of GUTs.

She did the best she could with what she had when it mattered the most. She gave me three great gifts: The gift of life, the gift of the wisdom to "be a light, not a judge," and the gift of knowing that love can get you through anything.

Mom got pregnant with me in the early 1960s and, in the midst of a very difficult situation, gave birth to me. It was not easy. She was in labor for over 72 hours, and the doctors thought I was dead. After finding my heart beat, they performed an emergency C-section and I was brought into this world.

Her prized possession was a four wheel drive International pickup truck. My mom loved that damn truck and lived in the back of it at times. More than once she dropped the old, broken-down transmission out of that truck by herself, then put in a new rebuilt transmission. Why? Because she could and she had to. She could not afford to pay someone to do it, so she did it herself. At that time, not many women—or men, for that matter—could do that sort of thing

As long as I can remember she worked three jobs at a time to provide for our family. She waitressed for 27 years. She did custom embroidery for the stars working on the strip in Las Vegas. She worked on food trucks—just about anything to help our little family survive.

We were poor and at times could not afford groceries. Sometimes Mom would get off work around 2 a.m. and get in that wonderful four wheel drive pickup and drive to the back of the supermarket where they kept the dumpsters. Here the stores would throw out the food that had just expired—vegetables that were going bad, milk, eggs, and meat that were past the expiration date. She'd dive into those dumpsters, gather the best pickings, take it home, clean it up, and make the most amazing stew you have ever tasted. We called it "dumpster stew," and wow, it tasted good.

Growing up on "dumpster stew" was a good thing for me and my family. I loved the taste of it. And when we would share it with friends they loved it too, until they found out the ingredients came from the trash. Through it all, Mom was bound and determined to take care of her family "come hell or high water," and I can tell you she definitely went through hell at times. But she always tried to live her life from her GUT, and it took GUTs to live the life she did.

She was not perfect and made many mistakes. Earlier in her life, she suffered from many poor choices. She would often get into abusive relationships that negatively impacted her and our family. When I, her oldest son, found my purpose and passion, she began to see how much better life can be when you make different choices. When I was in my mid-twenties, my mom started to change significantly.

Eventually she found a greater purpose and passion—a bold vision to bring her family together in love and unity. She wrote constantly and got her story published. As my family grew she shared her own wisdom with me. She started working on her family tree and became a fanatic about her family's peace and happiness. At last she knew what she wanted out of life, and why she wanted it.

She died early from complications of surgery. But when she died, she was settled, loved in her community and family, and happy. She became good at listening to her GUT telling her what was right and what wouldn't work.

At times she wondered if she could do it. But she had the GUTs to do it, and she did it.

Go With Your GUT!

Answer these questions for yourself. Write down your answers.

1. What are things that get in the way of change? Do you know people who have been successful in overcoming those obstacles to change? How did they do it?

2. What gets in your way when you want to change things in your own life?

3. What is your Big Why? Are you ready to follow the steps in this chapter and find it?

PART 2

Your GUT Instincts!

Understanding how to draw on the GUT, the brain, and the heart in fulfilling your life's purpose

CHAPTER 5

The Story of the GUT

The enteric or "GUT" nervous system is often called a "second brain." Hundreds of millions of GUT neurons communicate constantly with the primary brain. Let me tell you why this discovery makes a difference for your life.

When I was a kid, I remember feeling in my GUT that things just weren't right.

I grew up in an environment that was like a drug-crazed version of *The Brady Bunch* crossed with an episode of *COPS.* I was taught at a very young age that certain things were okay, even encouraged: "Be a bully, experiment with drugs and alcohol, aggressively pursue women sexually." Growing up I became a reflection of these teachings. I did not know anything but what my family taught me.

But something deep inside me was unsettled.

The problem was, my *GUT* knew what I was doing was wrong for me. I remember actually getting sick to my stomach when I would do things my family thought were perfectly acceptable.

"It Was Just a GUT Feeling"

It was a common sight for the U.S. soldiers patrolling Mosul, Iraq—a car parked by the roadside with a couple of young boys in it. The kids huddled together whispering as they watched the soldiers approach.

It was 120 degrees on a summer morning. Hardly anyone was in the marketplace. The windows of the car were rolled up. One of the soldiers was concerned that the boys would overheat inside the car and asked his sergeant if he could go help them, maybe help them out of the car and give them some water.

"No—no," the sergeant said. He had a hunch. "My body suddenly got cooler; you know, that danger feeling."

The soldiers had just enough time to back away from the car before it exploded, tossing them to the ground and killing the two boys.

Where did the sergeant's GUT feeling come from? "I can't point to one thing," he said later. "I just had that feeling you have."

Benedict Carey, "In Battle, Hunches Prove Valuable," New York Times, July 27, 2009.

I also remember a deep-down good feeling when I behaved like a person of dignity, honoring the law, and loving and serving others. Despite the crazy encouragement from my family to live a lawless life, something inside me rebelled. I discovered that I just felt better when I treated people with dignity and respect. My body felt stronger and my head clearer when I avoided drugs and alcohol. I felt more like a man when I respected the virtue of the young women I spent time with.

My GUT taught me things that my head didn't understand. Something in my GUT told me I would be good at football.

Something in my GUT told me it was better to treat people with kindness instead of bullying them.

Something in my GUT taught me to use my mind, to be curious, to learn and improve my grades.

Something in my GUT taught me to live a life worth living, to make a contribution, to become someone special, and to try to be a blessing in the lives of everyone I come in contact with.

The irony was that my GUT was guiding my head. And it was a good thing.

I have talked about finding your life's purpose. If I had followed what my head was telling me, I might have never found mine. My head was into sex, drugs, and rock and roll, but I *know* that I felt better when I tried to live in line with what my GUT was telling me. You might think it's crazy, but it's true.

Now we find out that the idea of a GUT feeling might be more than just a figure of speech. Scientists are now telling us we might have been right all along. Maybe the GUT does know something. You always hear people say things like "I had a GUT reaction" or "I just had a GUT feeling" or "it's a GUT instinct." You never hear them say "I had a spleen feeling" or "I just had this liver reaction" or "it's an instinct in my big toe."

Nope. It's always "in the GUT!"

Sometimes a GUT feeling seems to come from nowhere. Sometimes it hits you hard like a sudden insight, other times it's just a deep-down thing—we speak of a feeling that "something is off" or "not quite right." Sometimes we speak of a "nagging feeling" that "there must be more to life than this." Sometimes it's a feeling that saves your life.

For example, it was just a little brush fire in a gully when foreman Wag Dodge and his fifteen firefighters arrived at Mann Gulch in Montana. They thought it would be easy to put out, so they started working on it downhill with the wind at their backs.

Suddenly and without warning, the wind reversed and blew hard against them. The fire reversed course and exploded into a raging wall of flame called a "blow-up": it was now heading straight for the team. The men raced desperately for the top of the gully. Wag ran with them, but it was hopeless: the fire was coming too fast. He and his men were trapped, and he needed to do something else.

His GUT told him to do something totally unexpected—to set a fire in front of himself so that when the big flames arrived, there would be no fuel left to burn. He told his men what he was going to do, struck a match, and ignited the grass at their feet.

The escape fire blazed up the hill, and with only a minute to spare, Wag shouted, "Up this way!" But another squad leader said, "To hell with that; I'm getting out of here." Alone, Wag crouched inside his pocket of burned grass, and sure enough, the big fire went right around him. While thirteen men died in their hopeless race, Wag survived.

When he was later asked why he did what he did, he said the idea just came to him. He'd never heard of such a thing before. "Escape fires" are now a well-understood way to save lives in a grassfire situation.[21]

What Wag Dodge experienced was a GUT feeling based on years of fighting fires and a kind of deep intuition he had developed. The idea of an escape fire was totally counterintuitive, which is why his team didn't stay with him. Reason told them to run; but Wag's GUT told him otherwise. The odds shifted in his favor when he started listening to his GUT.

"We humans have known from time immemorial something that science is only now discovering: our GUT feeling is responsible in no small measure for how we feel. . . . Our self is created in our head and our GUT," says German scholar Giulia Enders. In other words, we need both brains and GUTS to guide our actions.

Why is this so? Well, for one thing, there *is* a brain in the GUT, or rather, a network of 100 million neurons similar to the billions of neurons in your head. Dr. Enders says, "There is only one other organ in the body that can compete with the GUT for diversity— the brain. The GUT's network of nerves is called the 'GUT brain' because it is just as large and chemically complex as the gray matter in our heads." [22]

---

21 This story is told in detail by Norman MacLean, Young Men and Fire, University of Chicago Press, 1992.

22 Enders, Giulia, GUT: The Inside Story of Our Body's Most Underrated Organ, Scribe Publications, 2015, 125.

"In comparison to the many billions of neurons in the brain, the GUT's hundreds of millions might not seem like much. And yet it's quite clear "GUT feelings" are no longer just a metaphor." [23]

"The GUT's network of nerves is called the "GUT brain" because it is just as large and chemically complex as the gray matter in our heads."

–Dr. Giulia Enders

The GUT and the brain talk to each other constantly. All day long the GUT sends signals upstream along a nerve called the vagus that connects to the brain, then the brain feeds back signals downstream through a second vagus nerve. So you can think of the GUT and the brain as two intelligences with a direct phone line to each other.

Furthermore, when the phone line reaches the brain, it branches out. The GUT can talk straight to different parts of the brain— including the centers of self-awareness, emotion, morality, fear, and motivation. It isn't that the GUT comes up with ideas the way the brain does, or that the GUT controls our thinking, but there's no doubt that it does *influence* our thinking.[24]

The reasoning part of our brain is very young, while the GUT is very, very old in terms of the past of the human family. The "GUT brain" probably evolved in order to help our ancestors survive and thrive. It appears to "sense" things that the higher brain misses. For example, we get a "GUT reaction" when we sense a threat, as our distant ancestors did when a tiger showed up. This reaction, says consultant and researcher Simone Wright, has come a long way from "There's a dangerous predator over there" to "This business deal doesn't feel right." [25] But it's basically the

---

23 Rathi, Akshat, "Science Says Your GUT Feeling Isn't Just a Metaphor," Quartz.com, August 10, 2015. http://qz.com/474523/is-your-GUT-really-the-second-brain/

24 Enders, 126.

25 Cited in Winfrey, Oprah, "What Oprah Knows for Sure About Trusting Her Intuition," O,

same thing, and could be what we mean when we talk about "GUT feelings." Your throat tightens up, or you feel a knot in your stomach, or you might even get physically ill. When we hear of something truly disturbing, we say it is "GUT-wrenching."

On the other hand, when you do something kind or generous or unselfish, it registers in your GUT, too. The GUT makes 95 percent of the serotonin in your body, the famous mood-balancing chemical that plays a role in feelings of well-being. Acts of kindness and generosity give you bursts of oxytocin and dopamine, the "bliss hormones" that help you feel contented and happy.

"People don't appreciate their intestines until something goes wrong. But I always hope that people gain a little appreciation for their GUTs."

–Mary Roach, science writer

It's no wonder that scientists are now so interested in this "second brain" in your body. Till recently, they ignored what was going on in the GUT. Now, prominent psychologists are turned on to what Jonathan Haidt calls "the moral GUT." Professor Dacher Keltner of Berkeley says that listening to the moral GUT "helps you trust and cooperate and share resources with others." [26]

If the moral GUT is "the source of our most important moral intuitions," as the researchers say, we have to listen to it if we're going to make our lives purposeful.

It's hard to describe a "GUT feeling." You know it if you've had it. Oprah Winfrey describes it as "a whispery sensation that pulsates just beneath the surface of your being." She also says,

---

The Oprah Magazine, August 2011. http://www.oprah.com/spirit/Oprah-on-Trusting-Her-Intuition-Oprahs-Advice-on-Trusting-Your-GUT

26 Keltner, Dacher, Born to Be Good: The Science of a Meaningful Life, W.W. Norton, 2009, ix, 47

"I've trusted the still, small voice of intuition my entire life, and the only time I've made mistakes is when I didn't listen." [27]

"Behold the proverbial "Aha!" Moment. In today's fast-paced industries, everyone is eager to foster these sparks of creativity, and it's no wonder why: From these "Aha!" Moments come world-changing breakthroughs."

–Lauren Migliore, science writer

Others describe the voice of the GUT as "a strong sensation . . . intuitive knowledge," as one woman described it when she finally found a house she wanted to buy. "The minute my realtor pulled up at the house, my body tingled with recognition." [28] Many people have experiences like that, where they "just know" that they will marry a certain person, or that their child will be a girl, and lo and behold, it happens. Has it happened to you?

More often, though, the GUT feeling comes when you're in a quiet state of mind. Scientists have monitored the brain waves of people who have sudden insights and found that in most cases the "aha!" moment comes while the person is daydreaming or taking a walk or a shower—in other words, when they're "zoned out." [29]

Maybe you've had that experience? You're just fooling around not doing much when all of a sudden you get this brilliant idea? It's happened to me. That's why I say you should give yourself some quiet space when you're trying to discover your inner purpose. Take a shower, go for a walk or a bike ride, take a

---

27 Winfrey, "What Oprah Knows."

28 Meadows, Charlson, "How Does Intuition Speak to Me?" Take Charge of Your Well Being, University of Minnesota blog, August 2006. http://www.takingcharge.csh.umn.edu/explore-healing-practices/intuition-healthcare/how-does-intuition-speak-me

29 Migliore, Lauren, "The Aha Moment: The Creative Science Behind Inspiration," BrainWorld Magazine, June 14, 2012.

notebook and a pencil and sit under a tree. Follow the process in this book.

Also, you need to unplug yourself from distractions and noise—especially the digital distractions—if you want to find your life purpose. You're not going to find it while you're online texting or watching TV or gaming. You've got to walk away from all that stuff—and from your day-to-day work, too. You can't be slamming away at the job and listen to this deep inner voice at the same time. Leave your phone home when you go sit under that tree.

But, you ask, what if my "GUT feelings" are wrong? What if my GUT says, "this is your life purpose," and it turns out to be a failure?

Good question. The first thing I would suggest is that maybe you aren't really in tune with that inner voice yet. Check your feelings again. Are you feeling afraid? Are you worried and stressed out about following your vision and purpose? Does it make you anxious? If so, you need to keep listening. You're not there yet.

There is some recent data showing that GUT insights are actually pretty trustworthy. Four different experiments reported in *Scientific American* showed that problems that were solved by sudden insight were correct 94 percent of the time, compared with 78 percent accuracy for solutions that were obtained by "analyzing the problem." [30]

According to psychologists who have studied GUT feelings, "they happen suddenly, they come easily, and they feel like positive experiences. And perhaps most importantly, they feel *right*—you assume they're true, even before you've had time to determine if that's actually the case." [31]

"GUT feelings . . . take advantage of the evolved capacities of the brain and are based on rules of thumb that enable us to act

---

30 Jacobson, Roni, "Can You Trust a Eureka Moment?" Scientific American Online, May 1, 2016. http://www.scientificamerican.com/article/can-you-trust-a-eureka-moment/

31 Romm, Cari, "Turns Out You Really Do Think Brilliant Thoughts in the Shower," New York Magazine, April 25, 2016.

fast and with astounding accuracy," says Dr. Gerd Gigerenzer, director of the Max Planck Institute for Human Development in Berlin. "GUT feelings can outwit the most sophisticated reasoning and computational strategies."

Why is this so? Because we make lots of decisions and we make them fast. We can't afford to analyze every decision we make or we would never have time to do anything else. Through day-to-day living, we have stockpiled enormous amounts of data that we are unconscious of, and a GUT decision draws on that stockpile.

For example, Dr. Gigerenzer asks, how does a baseball player catch a ball? The player doesn't compute the trajectory of the ball. He doesn't measure wind speed, air resistance, spin, the mass of the ball, or any of many other variables—he just watches the ball and catches it. How does he do this without a computer that has been programmed to do rapid-fire calculus? And if you ask him how he does it, he's likely to just tell you he doesn't know.

According to Gigerenzer, it's "GUT feel" that enables the player to catch a ball. The player doesn't need a lot of logic and mathematics and reasoning—in fact, it would probably

Have Faith in GUT Feelings

"The unfortunate thing we do in this culture is we try to tell people that intuition is illogical. I think intuition is the answer to the important questions.

"You've got to train yourself to listen to it, feel it and go with it.

"When you're working with people, you've got to help them to bring it out. You'll find the brilliance of people comes when you help them free themselves from this idea that you can't trust yourself."

–Bob Pittman, founder of MTV, CEO of iHeartMedia

[http://www.usatoday.com/story/money/business/2014/07/11/bob-pittman-clear-channel/12499617/]

just get in the way. GUT decisions are "fast and frugal." Less information is more.[32]

"GUT reactions and intuition . . . are neurologically based behaviors that evolved to ensure that we humans are able to respond in a split second when our survival is at stake."

–Dr. Gerd Gigerenzer, Max Planck Institute

We hear a lot about the "10,000 Hours" factor, the notion that you need 10,000 hours of deliberate practice to become a top performer in anything. But we all know people who *didn't* need the 10,000 hours—they were "born that way." They were catching baseballs with precision or singing beautifully or solving advanced puzzles when they were barely out of diapers.

And now it looks like the value of long years of "deliberate practice" may be overstated: A major Princeton study has found that prolonged practice "accounts for just a 12% difference in performance in various domains." [33] Could it be that "GUT feel" is just as important as or even more important than lots of practice? Could it be that your GUT is the key guide to what you should do with your life?

One thing the experts don't talk about but which I think is really important is the *joy* the player feels when the ball touches down firmly but softly into the glove. A beautiful catch in baseball is a joy to behold.

We all know people who are terrific at these kinds of GUT behaviors. The baseball player is one example. What about great cooks, singers, accountants, dealmakers, lawyers, or engineers? They "just know" when it works, don't they?

---

32 Gigerenzer, Gerd, GUT Feelings: The Intelligence of the Unconscious, Penguin Group, 2008.

33 Baer, Drake, "New Study Destroys 10,000 Hour Rule," Business Insider, July 3, 2014. http://www.businessinsider.com/new-study-destroys-malcolm-gladwells-10000-rule-2014-7

There's that baker who can give you his recipe for a cake, but you'll never be able to reproduce what he does—not because he's falsified the recipe, but because he can't really explain how he makes it "great." "You just *feel* when it's right," he says. "It's a GUT feeling."

There's the airline pilot who puts down a giant airliner on a runway and the passengers feel nothing, just a whisper of the wheels touching the ground. It's a perfect landing. How does she do it? She can't tell you. "It's a GUT thing."

There's that teacher you remember who had a "feeling" for teaching, or that mechanic who could "feel" what your car needed, or that manager you once had with the uncanny "feel" for making the right decisions.

Do those people get satisfaction out of what they do? Absolutely! It's a major source of joy in life—to fulfill with excellence the great purpose that they were born to fulfill.

Everyone—including you—has that potential great purpose deep down inside.

Does your life purpose give you chills (the good kind)? Do you feel deep-down excited? Now that you know your life's purpose, do you think that in all the future mornings of your life you'll get up eager to get at it? If so, then you *are* in touch with that inner voice that tells you about that purpose.

I love the word "eager." It's not the same as "anxious," even though we use it that way sometimes. "Anxious" isn't happy—the word is full of fear, worry, cold sweats, and dread. If you feel anxious, it's your GUT telling you to step back and think again.

"Eager" is the opposite. "Eager" is happy—the word is full of enthusiasm, zest, energy, and impatience. If you feel eager, it's your GUT telling you that you're on the right track. It's not in your imagination—it's in your *body*. It's in your GUT!

I give a lot of public speeches. Do I feel "anxious" before I give one? Well, I sweat and tremble and get butterflies in my stomach like anybody else—but it is *not* primarily from anxiety. It's from *eagerness*. I'm raring to get up there and can't wait for my turn.

I want to live an eager life, not an anxious life. What about you?

People who won't listen to that deep, purposeful voice end up with a lot of negative thought patterns, such as "I'm worthless," or "it's no use," or "nothing ever works out for me." Giulia Enders points out that "the nervous messages from a worried GUT can also become embedded in a person's mind" [34]—and you don't want that.

The day I pulled myself up from the dirt of a junior high school track in Las Vegas I knew my life's purpose. I heard it deep down. I knew what my contribution would be. I knew it would not be a life wasted on careless sexual exploits and the living death of drugs and alcohol.I also knew it would not be a life with no focus or reason other than getting through the day. I would create a life of purpose and meaning and giving to others. All this came welling up inside of me.

On that day I became eager for the future. On that day the odds that were stacked against me shifted in my favor.

If you think about tomorrow and it gives you a stomach ache, could it be that your GUT is trying to tell you something?

As one scholar says, "Intuition is a master teacher about life when we are willing students." [35] We have to be willing to listen to what the GUT is telling us—and we have to be willing to follow that voice.

---

34 Enders, 138.
35 Meadows, "How Does Intuition Speak?"

Go With Your GUT!

Answer these questions for yourself. Write down your answers.

1. Have you ever felt like you "just know" something is right? When has this happened to you?

2. Can you tell the difference between being "anxious" and being "eager"? Do you feel more anxious or more eager about your future? Why?

3. Do you have thoughts like "I'm worthless," or "it's no use," or "nothing ever works out for me"? When you think like that, what do you feel in your GUT?

4. How can you tell if your "GUT feeling" about your life's purpose is right or wrong?

CHAPTER 6

How to Use Your GUT Instinct

We draw on our GUT instincts when we face tough decisions. In this chapter we talk about the "how"—the skill of calling on your GUT feelings to guide your thinking. We also talk about the skill of "GUT checking" our decisions after we make them.

Okay, now we've talked about GUT instinct, why it's so important to you, and where it comes from. Now let's talk about how to tap into and *use* your GUT instinct when you have important decisions to make, like these: "What's my future? What about my career? What about my relationships? What should my life be about?"

These are big choices to make. How can you use GUT instinct in making them?

Study first. First of all, don't base all your decisions on GUT instinct. For example, if you've got a whole lot of options in front of you ("Should I get a job? Should I quit my job? Should I go back to school? Should I go to Alaska and take pictures of bears?"), please do your "due diligence" first. By that I mean you should study each option—download into your head all the useful facts you can find. Talk to knowledgeable people you trust. If the answer isn't clear to your reasoning mind after you've done that, then your GUT instinct comes into play.

Ponder. Go for a walk in a calm and serene environment, like a park early in the morning or a grove or a desert place. It's important not to have a lot of outside distractions. Or find a quiet place and meditate. There are many meditation techniques—practice and use a meditation technique that works for you. The key is to clear your mind of other cares and concerns. (I have co-written with Dr. Michael Olpin a more detailed book on this subject: *Unwind: 7 Principles for a Stress-Free Life,* Grand Harbor Press, 2014.)

Listen to the first answer. Ask yourself the big question that's bothering you and then listen. Often your intuition is faster than your reasoning mind, so the first answer you hear might be the best one.

When you tap into your GUT instinct, you're listening to all the wisdom of your body, which, as we've seen, *knows* a lot. As a result of untold ages of development, the body senses threats. It can "smell" danger not only to your physical well-being but also to your emotional and social well-being.

That's why you hear women say, "He seemed all right, but my GUT told me there was something wrong." Small signals that don't register with our brains often register with the GUT—maybe the guy stands just a little too close or there's something indefinable in his eyes. Or you hear a friend say, "It looked like a really good job opportunity, but it just didn't feel right." You pick up on hints and clues without being conscious of them—they're just feelings you can't define.

The GUT instinct is often very fast. You *feel* the answer before you know it. Obviously, you're going to have many possible solutions, and they're all racing to the foreground of your mind. But which one got to the gate first?

We all know about "first impressions." You meet a person and you size them up, well, it seems almost instantly. And it *is* almost instant. According to the experts, it takes just ten milliseconds, or one-tenth of a second, to form an impression of a stranger.[36] That makes sense because our bodies are programmed for quick self-defense. Our ancestors were the ones who figured out pretty fast if a stranger was a threat or not; the slow ones didn't live long enough to be our ancestors.

"GUT feelings don't seem entirely rational," says the celebrated author Malcolm Gladwell, who wrote a whole book on the subject. He tells numerous stories about "the first two seconds"—the time it takes to experience a GUT reaction. The GUT reaction might not seem to make sense at first, Gladwell concedes, "but I think that what goes on in those first two seconds is perfectly rational. It's thinking—it's just thinking that moves a little faster and operates a little more mysteriously than the kind of deliberate, conscious decision-making that we usually associate with 'thinking'.

"The key to good decision-making is not knowledge. It is understanding. We are swimming in the former. We are desperately lacking in the latter.

"If we are to learn to improve the quality of the decisions we make, we need to accept the mysterious nature of our snap judgments." [37]

---

36 Todorov, Alexander and Janine Willis, "First Impressions," Psychological Science, 17 (2006), 598.

37 Gladwell, Malcolm, Blink: The Power of Thinking

The Power of Pondering

"Somewhere, something exciting is waiting to be known," said Carl Sagan. Often that "somewhere" is inside you. But you won't discover it without pondering it. Have you ever pondered the power of pondering?

The word "ponder" has many cool synonyms: "To think about, contemplate, consider, review, reflect on, mull over, meditate on, muse on, deliberate about, cogitate on, dwell on, brood on, ruminate on, chew over, puzzle over, turn over in one's mind."

If you don't take time to ponder what your GUT is telling you, you might as well not listen at all. Pondering is a great habit to get into. By the way, pondering can save you from dementia as you age, according to the McGill Center for Studies in Aging.

Neale McDevitt, "The PONDER Project: Using Your Brain to Ward Off Dementia," Med-E News, 2012.

Check your GUT. Mull over that first answer that got to the gate before any other thoughts. Test it by flipping a coin: "Should I do A or B?" Now pay close attention to your GUT reaction. Does it feel uncomfortable down there? Or does the GUT feel happy? Professor William Ickes at the University of Texas has experimented with the coin toss: "If I'm happy with the way the coin toss came out, I go with that. If I'm disappointed with the way the coin toss came out, I ignore its outcome and choose the other alternative." [38]

You can also "try on the decision," like trying on a new shirt or pair of shoes. The famous psychotherapist Dr. Karol Ward suggests picturing your future if you make choice A or choice B. Picture both the positive and negative things about each choice. Think of yourself in the fitting room at a dress shop. Look in the mirror. Does that decision "fit"? How does your GUT feel? Do you feel "muscle tightness or pain (or in extreme cases actual illness)"? Or do you feel "pleasant sensations, like tingling or fluttering, a sense of warmth in the chest, or a flush of excitement that runs from the toes to the head"?

A consultant to all the major TV networks, Dr. Ward talks about the "GUT check" quite often. The best decision almost always causes excitement deep down, while the poor decision can literally make us sick.

Still, we reason ourselves into poor decisions. Why? Could be several reasons. We're too lazy to do the due diligence up front. We're over-dependent on somebody else to make decisions for us. We're locked into things that have worked in the past and we refuse to learn new things. We never do the "GUT check."

"We talk ourselves out of trusting our 'GUT' because it doesn't always jibe with what's in our heads," Dr. Ward says. "When our body tells us one thing and our mind another, we can feel stuck or paralyzed when it comes to making a decision. But nine times out of 10, we fall back on that familiar, logical mind. Yet, from

---

Without Thinking, Little, Brown, 2007.

38 Mathison, Susan, "The Science of a GUT Feeling," PositivelyBeautiful.com, August 2, 2012.

what others share with me, nine times out of 10, going with the mind ends up being a big mistake."

"Countless times my clients have said to me, 'I knew it. I knew I shouldn't have made the choice I did because it didn't *feel* right. But I did it anyway. I talked myself into it.' Almost without fail, when I've asked what they meant by 'didn't feel right,' they could pinpoint a sensation in their bodies, a physical clue that something was wrong." [39]

"Trusting your GUT is trusting the collection of all your subconscious experiences."

–Dr. Melody Wilding, Hunter College

I have a friend who made the most important decision of his life one day: He got engaged to a young woman. It made perfect sense. They had dated for more than a year. They knew each other well. They had a lot of the same interests, the same kind of job, the same faith. They loved the same movies, the same music, the same foods, everything. They had lots of the same friends. They were attracted to each other. They did argue sometimes, but don't most couples? It just seemed like a natural thing to do.

But after the engagement, he went home and was almost overwhelmed with a feeling deep down that it just wasn't right. "I sat down on the floor in my unfurnished room, turned off the lights, and suffered. I was sick to my stomach. I felt like a weight was sitting on top of my head." Finally, he got talking to his mother—a wise woman—who could tell he wasn't happy. He admitted to her that the whole engagement thing was making him sick, and she suggested maybe he had made the wrong choice.

---

39 Ward, Karol, Find Your Inner Voice: Using Instinct and Intuition Through the Body-Mind Connection, New Page Books, 2009, 41.

"But," he said, "it makes so much sense!" His brain was fighting his GUT. At last he gave in to his GUT, broke off the engagement, and almost immediately felt a huge sense of relief. He wasn't sick anymore.

Now, lest you think this guy was just allergic to making commitments, it wasn't more than a month later that he met another young woman. Ironically, she was a lot like the first one—a great cook, a movie buff, smart, and talented. He dated the second young woman for about a year too.

But this time, it was totally different. "I felt warm and excited about her. I kept asking myself why I was feeling so peaceful. I was even afraid that those other awful feelings would come back, but they never did." The GUT check was positive this time. They got engaged and have had a happy marriage now for quite a few years. When I get together with them, I can feel that they are right for each other.

My friend can't explain why the first engagement didn't work and the second one did. Neither can I, and neither can you. There was nothing wrong with the first woman. Both women were great people. But it was my friend's GUT feeling that guided him in the right direction *for him*.

Such an important decision might just depend on how your GUT feels about it.

But are GUT decisions always right? Of course not, but they're often better than slow, deliberate decisions even when the question is messy or complicated. In Gladwell's book, he tells of a research project where a group of people were asked to select a new car based on four features. A second group had to choose a car based on twelve features. Both groups were asked to use "deliberative thought" in making their choices. The first group made good choices, but the second group made poor choices. With too much to think about, the question was too complicated to wrap their brains around.

Professor Ed Cohen suggests that there is a "wisdom of the GUT." *"We are more than we know*," he says, "for when it comes from the GUT, intelligence does not take the form of knowledge."[40]

The evidence even says that we need the GUT in order to make *any* decision. A study of brain-damaged people who lost touch with their "emotional intuitions" reports that they had to use only reasoning to decide on anything. "They ended up doing such complicated analysis, factoring everything in, that it could take them hours to decide between two kinds of cereal." [41]

So it's not only a good idea but basic good sense to listen to your GUT when you have important decisions to make.

When should you not trust your GUT?

Some people go to the other extreme, always "going with the GUT." But just because an idea *feels* right doesn't mean that it *is* right. That's why you need to do your "due diligence" first. That's why you need to load up with

40 Cohen, Ed, "GUT Wisdom, or Why We Are More Intelligent Than We Know," Somatosphere.net, October 21, 2013.

41 Flora, Carlin, "GUT Almighty!" Psychology Today, May 1, 2007.

Imagination, Intuition, and Insight: Where From?

"Our deep understanding of analytical reasoning tells us nothing about the extraordinary mental processes of imagination, intuition, and insight that underlie many forms of creative thinking: the sudden flash of inspiration; the surprising emergence of a meaningful pattern in the midst of complexity; the insightful reframing of a problem; the leap to a whole new space of ideas."

Professor Richard Ogle, University of North Carolina

the best facts and counsel you can get. That's why you need to test out your GUT instincts.

Nobody believes that pure GUT instinct always produces a better solution than sound, well-informed thinking. "The second brain doesn't help with the great thought processes . . . religion, philosophy and poetry is left to the brain in the head," according to Dr. Michael Gershon at Columbia University Medical Center.[42] Obviously, nothing takes the place of homework when you're making an important decision.

But the thing I love about "going with your GUT" is the excitement I feel when it tells me to feel excited. I know that sounds weird, but I live by that eager, thrilling feeling that comes from deep down inside when I know I'm living my life's purpose. I can live it with gusto! I try to do my homework, but my real zest in life comes from the life vision that my GUTS tell me is right for me.

Go With Your GUT!

Answer these questions for yourself. Write down your answers.

1. When did you make an important decision that "didn't feel right"? Why or why not?

2. Have you had "first impressions" about people? When did they turn out to be right – or wrong?

3. What are some things to watch out for when you're listening to your GUT instincts?

4. What big questions are you facing right now? Are you ready to follow the steps in this chapter to find answers?

---

42 Hadhazy, Adam, "Think Twice: How the GUT's 'Second Brain' Influences Mood and Well-Being," Scientific American, February 12, 2010.

CHAPTER 7

Trusting Your GUT—Balanced With Your Head and Heart

GUT instinct is essential, but must be part of a "three-legged stool" of GUT, brain, and heart. The neuron mesh in the brain on your shoulders is "the most complicated object in the known universe." [43] *The heart, which also contains neurons, is far more complex than we think and is in constant "conversation" with the brain. Here's how you keep your balance on that three-legged stool so you can make the choices that lead to a full and successful life.*

"What if I don't trust my GUT?"

It's important to balance your GUT feelings against what your heart tells you and what your head tells you. Most of us listen too much to one of those sources of wisdom without listening to them all.

If I listen too much to my HEAD, I end up deciding what to do based only on logic and reason. These are important things. But what if, say, Steve "Woz" Wozniak—the inventor of the personal computer—had listened to his father? When he was in junior high, Steve told his dad, an electrical engineer, that someday he would

---

43 Cited in "Behold the Most Complicated Object in the Known Universe," The Leonard Lopate Show, February 25, 2014. http://www.wnyc.org/story/michio-kaku-explores-human-brain/

"own his own computer." His dad told him, "No way. Those things cost as much as a house." [44] If he had listened only to his head, Woz would never have tried to build the first personal computer.

If I listen too much to my HEART, I end up deciding what to do based only on emotion. My feelings are important. But what if, say, you or your parents or your grandparents had decided not to risk loving someone enough to have a child with them?

"The greatest risk is the risk of riskless living."

–Stephen R. Covey

I believe most people are okay with listening to the HEAD or the HEART, but they're not used to listening to the GUT. Yet it's often what the GUT tells you that enables you to strike the right balance between HEAD and HEART.

For 35 years I kept secret the challenges I had as a child. The strange and freaky environment I lived in growing up, the abuse, the drug use, the homelessness—all a secret. I was ashamed of the way I was raised.

But through a bold vision, finding my purpose, hard work, and the help of a few key people along the way, I made it out of a very difficult childhood and became a successful adult with my own great career path and beautiful family. Because of the great sense of gratitude I have for the wonderful blessing I have in my life, I have always tried to give back.

Some years ago I volunteered as a counselor at a maximum-security youth prison for really troubled kids, many of whom came out of the same kind of background I did. Every week I spent countless hours working with the kids. I knew what they needed

---

44 Chen, Brian X., "Steve Wozniak's 9 Favorite Gadgets," Wired.com, December 6, 2010. https://www.wired.com/2010/12/steve-wozniak-favorite-gadgets/

to do to change their lives and I told them so. The problem was that they did not care about what I told them. They did not trust me or my motives, even though my intentions where really good.

After a year of sacrifice and hard work with these kids, one evening I came home frustrated because my GUT told me I was making no difference in the lives of these troubled youth. So I reached out to my trusted confidant and best friend, my wife Kim, and I asked her what I was doing wrong. In my heart I loved these kids, and I wanted nothing more than to help them on their journey the way so many had helped me.

She calmly listened to me and heard every word—she let me "bitch it out," so to speak, until I was done complaining. Then she looked into my eyes and lovingly asked me this question: "Sam have you taken the time to really listen to these kids, to understand their world and the challenges they are facing"?

"No," I said.

"At the right time, in the right circumstance, and with the right motivation, have you shared with them the challenges you had as a kid?"

"Oh, hell no," I said. "I don't want anyone to know what I went through as a kid. I have worked my entire life to keep that a secret." I thought it brought shame to myself and my family.

Then my best friend gave me this beautiful insight. "Honey, until you understand the kids' stories, and at the right time share your story and then serve them with all your HEART, you will be wasting your time. They can smell out a fake from miles away, so they need to hear what you have been through—that you're the real deal. You have this amazing gift of empathy to understand what most of these kids have gone through, and you are not even using it. Go back and *open your HEART!* Let go of fear and shame, listen to them, share who you really are with them, serve and love them, and then report back to me how it goes."

Well, I did exactly what Ms. Kim suggested, and everything changed. I had been using my HEAD on them—reasoning, logic, arguing, persuading, analyzing, debating—and all the time my GUT was telling me it wasn't enough. But when I shared my HEART with them—my pain as well as my love for them—my relationships with these troubled young people were transformed. They opened up to me, and together we grew into better people. They were the reason I wrote my first book, *My Orange Duffel Bag: A Journey to Radical Change*. Many people have told me how they were helped through radical changes in their lives by that book.

When you're confused or undecided or not sure what path to take in life, as I've said, you need to listen to your GUT. It doesn't take the place of rational thinking. But it's happened to me so often that I can't deny it—my GUT tells me what's going on with me.

"The embryo develops from three tubes: the brain comes from one tube, the heart from the second, and the GUT from the third."

–Dr. Giulia Enders

And it's true of the young people I work with. There are all races, backgrounds, religions, sizes, shapes, and skin colors—but they all have one thing in common. They really struggle to find happiness. Some overeat, sleep too much, or worry too much about their appearance. Others take terrible risks, like taking drugs, sleeping around, or joining gangs. Many of them are so miserable that life doesn't feel like it's worth living.

They also have something else in common: Deep down in the GUT they know what their problem is. They know that what they're doing isn't working for them. They squelch that calmer voice that you hear when you do what's right, when you're making good decisions and taking the upward way to a great life instead of the downward way to a miserable life.

A friend of mine, a great teacher, was once invited to speak to a college fraternity about "values." (It seems that the college was upset with the guys in the fraternity because they were acting a little too much like the crazy boys in the movie *Animal House*.)

Anyway, as he spoke, he asked them a serious question: "What kind of a man do you want to be?" They mocked him and made fun of the question. "Do you really think it's okay to take advantage of women?" he asked. "Do you really think it's okay to drink yourselves stupid every weekend? Do you *really* want to be that kind of person?"

They all laughed and shouted that that was exactly the kind of people they wanted to be.

So my friend gave them a little challenge, saying something like this. "Just do one thing for me. Sit there quietly for five minutes without talking. Close your eyes. Now think about my question again.

"What kind of a man do you want to be?"

They took him up on the challenge and silenced themselves for five minutes. They closed their eyes. They thought about his questions. There was a little giggling at first, but then the room got quieter and quieter.

At the end of the five minutes, he asked them, "Now how do you feel about my questions?"

One by one, hesitating at first, many of them admitted that they did *not* want to be that kind of person. They started talking seriously about how they'd been behaving around women, about stopping the "stupid" binge-drinking parties they'd been having. They started talking about their future. The whole atmosphere in the room changed.

Why? Because my friend got them to shut up and listen to the GUT. He knew that deep down inside was another voice, but they needed to be quiet in order to hear it.

He could have given them the standard lecture on STDs and sexual violence on campus and alcohol poisoning and drug addiction and all the horrors that are usually trotted out in those kinds of meetings. He could have put up charts and graphs or pictures of dead addicts or terrible drunk-driving accidents.

But he didn't do any of that. He knew they already knew all of that. Their heads were full of it, but it hadn't made a difference yet. Don't get me wrong—all of those horrors *are* horrors and very much a reality that those guys needed to face and really understand.

But he decided to talk not to the heads of those fraternity men, but to their GUTS and their HEARTS. Only then did it all come together for them and motivate them to change.

Let's find out how GUTsy you are when it comes to sex, drugs, and alcohol. Here's a little quiz:

SEX AND GUTS

True or false?

1. A person who dresses in tight or skimpy clothes should not be surprised if he / she is raped.

2. A person who goes into an assailant's room assumes the risk of sexual violence. (S/he should have known not to go in that place.)

3. Pornography is harmless.

4. A person who sexually teases someone else deserves whatever happens to him / her.

5. Sexual assault is often the result of miscommunication or a mistake.

108

6. If a drunk person is raped, that person is at least partly responsible for the rape.

7. If a person is willing to make out with someone, then it's no big deal if it goes on to sex.

8. If a person who is raped didn't fight back, it isn't rape.

9. A lot of women lead a man on and then cry rape.

10. When women say no, they really mean yes.

I am   1) Not likely   2) Pretty unlikely   3) Could go one way or the other   4) Pretty likely   5) Very likely to do the following:

11. Have sex with someone outside of my marriage.

12. Encourage a friend to talk to a counselor or an authority if they had an unwanted sexual experience.

13. Have a sexual relationship with more than one person.

14. Let someone who is being threatened with sexual abuse know that I am available to help.

15. Speak up if I hear someone say "She/He deserved to be raped."

16. Speak up if I think someone is being or has been sexually assaulted.

17. Have casual sex without being married.

18. Try to stop a person (even a friend) who is harassing someone.

19. Look at pornography.

20. Convince someone who is resistant to have sex with me.

Take 5 points for each correct true or false answer for questions 1-10. Key: 1F 2F 3F 4F 5F 6F 7F 8F 9F 10F

Reverse score on 11, 13, 17, 19, 20.

Enter your score here: _____

If your score is...	Then...
91-100	When it comes to sex, it takes GUTs to respect yourself and other people, to keep faith when you have made solemn promises, to stand up for people who are being abused—and you have GUTs!
81-90	You're not as serious as you ought to be about sexual abuse and harassment. You don't take your own solemn promises too seriously, and you lack the GUTs and the discipline to behave yourself consistently.
71-80	You probably like to pretend that casual sex is no big deal, that other people's bodies are there for your pleasure, or that a little sexual harassment is harmless. Deep down you know this isn't true.
0-70	No GUTs. You have little respect for yourself and other people. You tend to see them as sex objects. You take solemn promises lightly. You might even believe that sex-crime victims are asking for it. You need help!

What does your score mean?

In our society, it takes GUTs to respect the lives and bodies of others. With all the pornography out there, it takes GUTs not to turn into a voyeur on the internet. With all the casual attitudes about sex, it takes GUTs to be faithful to the promises made to a wife or husband. With the epidemic of sexual abuse and even rape on our campuses and our streets and even in our homes, it takes GUTs to stand up and stop it.

A guy who drools over porn or uses women for his own pleasure or cheats on his wife is GUTLESS. If he stops and ponders what he's really doing, deep down inside his GUT will tell him that what he's doing is just wrong.

The whole country was shocked when one night a champion member of the Stanford University swim team dragged an unconscious, intoxicated woman behind a dumpster and raped her. When a couple of students came on the scene, they put a stop to it right there, comforted the victim, and held the guy until the police arrived.

The swimmer was a disciplined athlete, even an Olympic prospect. But in my book he's GUTless.

On the other hand, the two men who stopped the whole thing, a couple of Swedish students, have real GUTs. They could have walked past and kept out of it. They could have, but didn't. Deep down inside, they knew they couldn't. When asked why they intervened, one of the students said, "I think it happened on instinct for us. I never thought about it twice and I'm glad I did it." [45] They listened to their GUTs.

Besides illicit sex, another GUTless behavior is alcohol and drug abuse. Four in ten college students have been drunk in the last month and 35 percent of them on a binge (five or more drinks in a row). Daily marijuana use has tripled in the last 20 years. About 10 percent of college students use cocaine or other illegal drugs.

Let's find out how GUTsy you are about drugs and alcohol.

DRUGS AND GUTS

True or false?

1. I can only fit in if I drink alcohol.

2. It can't be a party without alcohol.

---

45 Friedman, Megan, "One of the Students Who Stopped Brock Turner Describes the Horrible Scene He Saw," Cosmopolitan, June 8, 2016. http://www.cosmopolitan.com/college/a59595/carl-fredrik-arndt-interviews-stanford-assault-case/

3. Marijuana is harmless.

4. Marijuana is not as bad for your health as tobacco is.

5. People can get addicted to marijuana.

6. People who slip back into drug abuse after treatment are hopeless.

7. Rehab is a lifelong effort for most recovering addicts.

8. Using marijuana can cause learning problems.

9. You have to hit "rock bottom" before treatment will work.

10. You have to want treatment for it to succeed.

I am   1) Not likely   2) Pretty unlikely   3) Could go one way or the other   4) Pretty likely   5) Very likely to do the following:

11. Decline an alcoholic drink.

12. Drink too much.

13. Participate in binge-drinking parties.

14. Make sure that a friend who is intoxicated on alcohol or drugs gets home safely.

15. Refuse to take drugs that a doctor has not prescribed for me.

16. Smoke marijuana.

17. Speak up if a friend has a drug and/or alcohol problem.

18. Try a new kind of drug if it is offered to me.

19. Try to stop a friend from getting intoxicated on alcohol or drugs.

20. Use drugs that are not prescribed for me.

Take 5 points for each correct true or false answer for questions 1-10. Key: 1F 2F 3F 4F 5T 6F 7T 8T 9F 10F

Reverse score on 12, 13, 16, 18, 20.

Enter your score here: _____

If your score is...	Then...
91-100	It takes GUTs to lead a drug-free life in this society, and you have GUTs!
81-90	You need to get better informed about the dangers of drugs and make a few GUTsy decisions for yourself.
71-80	You don't yet know much about the risks of drugs and alcohol, which puts you at serious risk.
0-70	No GUTs. Your risky behavior and lack of knowledge make you an easy victim of the drugs-and-alcohol culture. Get some help!

A lot of kids smoke or drink or take drugs in order to show their friends that they have GUTs. This is very ironic (I was going to say, "This is B____ S_____"), because it takes a lot *more* GUTs to refuse that stuff. It takes the *opposite* of GUTs to fall for those destructive, addictive habits.

Look, none of this stuff is harmless, even marijuana. It can be as bad as or worse than tobacco because it's smoked differently. Marijuana smokers inhale more deeply, so they take in more toxins and tar. [46] Those who give in to the pressure to use this stuff and other drugs and keep using have no GUTs. Meanwhile, those struggling with addiction who seek rehab show real GUTs, especially if they keep trying even when they fail.

---

[46] "Marijuana and Lung Health," American Lung Association. http://www.lung.org/stop-smoking/smoking-facts/marijuana-and-lung-health.html?referrer=https://www.google.com/

I was touched by one teenager's comments on his blog. He has a caring mom and dad, but his dad is addicted to alcohol: "I've grown up with an alcoholic father. I remember thinking, when I was little, that everyone had a father that got drunk every night . . . I've never felt the pull of alcohol or drugs. Maybe it's because of the people I've surrounded myself with and learned to trust, and I think, *That's not who I want to become.* It's about the people your heart decides to care about and how they will be affected by your actions."

This boy stays free of drugs and alcohol not only because they're bad for him, but because his heart tells him to do so. What is your heart telling *you*? Who do *you* want to become?

People have always talked about "listening to your heart." It's an age-old notion, and there's a lot to it. When you're trying to decide what to do, if you're smart, your head is full of data, and that's good. But we all know that we don't always do what we know we should do. We know that if we value our health and our lives we should eat right, exercise, and avoid drugs and alcohol. Most of us still won't do these things even though we know we should. For example, about 16 percent of Americans smoke. Do you imagine those people don't know what it's doing to them?

Everybody knows how bad this stuff is. So your head isn't enough. You've got to listen to your heart *and* your GUT.

What do I mean by listening to your heart?

A well-known psychologist, Dr. Deborah Rozman, used to ask patients who were struggling with an important decision, "What would your heart say?" She would actually put the person in one chair and ask them to "speak from the heart" to the other chair, which represented the mind.

"Then I'd have them switch chairs and speak from the head, talking to the heart, telling the heart the mind's views and concerns. It was like two different people talking." She would have them switch chairs several times until they got used to listening to the voice of the heart—a voice of "intuition and common sense intelligence." She says that the heart speaks the language of "genuine feeling." [47]

It might be interesting for you to try this. Ask yourself, "What does my head say?" Then "What does my heart say?" Then "What does my GUT say?" You might even try sitting in different chairs. My bet is that you will hear three different answers, almost as if you were listening to three different people talking.

When you have an important choice to make, ask yourself, "What does my head say?" Then "What does my heart say?" Then "What does my GUT say?"

All three perspectives are important. Personally, I think the deciding answer comes from the GUT. Here's why.

The head, as we've said, gives you all the logic, facts, opinions, data—all the reasonable, rational stuff. This stuff is important. It's about doing your homework, finding out what's what. It's about knowing and facing the realities. In our society, we say that all good decisions require careful thought, and we're right about that. We need a rock-hard foundation in knowledge.

However, more is needed. Knowledge is usually not enough to change people's behavior. Otherwise we wouldn't smoke, overeat, drink too much, cheat, steal, lie, fight, or do all the other stupid and self-defeating things we do. In my case I know exercise is good for me. But it's really easy not to do it, believe me.

---

47 Rozman, Deborah, "Let Your Heart Talk to Your Brain," Huffington Post, February 11, 2013. http://www.huffingtonpost.com/heartmath-llc/heart-wisdom_b_2615857.html

"The heart is more than just a simple pump. The neurons in the heart enable it to make functional decisions independent of the workings of the brain in your head. . . . The heart brain influences perception, cognition and emotions."

–Dr. Gregory Stebbins, leadership consultant

The heart speaks from a different place. So kids do dumb things— their mothers still love them. (I was bad enough as a kid that *only* my mother could love me.) We love a lot of things for no particular reason: home, country, a song, a car, a TV show, a friend.

Scientists now know that there are neurons in the heart. "Just like the brain in our cranium has left and right hemispheres, our heart has a brain comprised of two nodes," according to psychologists Rosemary Sword and Philip Zimbardo. "Much more than just a pump, it conducts the cellular symphony that is the very essence of our being. And the heart has a memory stored in its muscles, just like our brain stores our daily experiences." [48]

"The heart sends more information to the brain than the brain sends to the heart; its rhythms affect our perception and the brain's ability to process information. . . . The signals the heart sends to the brain can affect our emotional experiences."

The brain carries on a conversation with the heart, but the heart might be saying even more to the brain. Whether the "heart brain" really is a center of emotion or just a metaphor, I've found that I can talk from my heart, whether it's to another person or, even more important, to myself.

So if your heart isn't into exercise, you might do it, but you won't get the emotional charge that exercise can give you.

So the head gives you logic and data. The heart gives you love. But the GUT gives you will-power, determination, and joy in the effort. That's why I think the GUT is the deciding voice. When

---

48 Sword, Rosemary K.M. and Philip Zimbardo, "Stress and Your Heart," Psychology Today blog, April 27, 2016.

your head says exercise, but you won't do it—and when your heart isn't in it—listen to that voice deep down that says you've *got to do it.* That's what it means to have GUTs.

HEAD · GUT · HEART

So how do I listen to my heart?

Here is what works for me.

I soften myself up. I think about the people who love me and who I love. I try to fill myself with compassion for myself and for others. I breathe deeply. Then I speak—either silently or aloud, if I'm alone. I try to stay close to my feelings. Rather than arguing with myself or trying to persuade myself of something, I just let out what I feel. I say what needs to be said. Sometimes it takes a long time; sometimes it all comes out fast. Sometimes I need a lot of words; sometimes I don't.

But I always benefit from hearing what my heart has to say. I understand that "feelings aren't facts," but they are very important to consider when making decisions. It's what I'm feeling. If there's a big rope around my heart—and there often is—I know I really need to loosen it and let the heart talk.

It's important to hear the voices of both mind and heart when you have an important decision to make. We are not just thinking creatures: we are also feeling creatures.

Now, in my opinion, it's wise to take both into account. But, as I've said before, the "GUT check" is the decider for me. In making decisions, my GUT gives me the best possible edge. I depend on the "three-legged stool" of brain, heart, and GUT.

I agree with the writer Michael LeGault: "The technique by which we make good decisions is a nuanced and interwoven mental process involving bits of emotion, observation, intuition, and critical reasoning. . . . The essential background to all this is a solid base of knowledge."[49]

In other words, we need it all—the critical reasoning of the head, the emotions of the heart, and the intuition of the GUT.

Go With Your GUT!

Answer these questions for yourself. Write down your answers.

1. When have you made a decision but your heart just wasn't in it?

2. Do you know what it feels like to speak from the heart? When has this worked for you?

3. Do you make choices based on pure mental reasoning or pure emotion? How is that working out for you?

4. What decisions do you need to make that you've been putting off? How about trying the "three-legged stool" approach?

5. What decisions have you made about your own character? Think about your scores on the quizzes in this chapter. Does your GUT tell you that your scores are good enough—or do you need to improve?

---

49 LeGault, Michael R., Think!: Why Crucial Decisions Can't Be Made in the Blink of an Eye, Simon & Schuster, 2006, 12.

PART 3

GUT IT OUT!

Pushing past failure and enjoying the journey

CHAPTER 8

Taking Off

You are clear on your destination—the reason for the journey—and your tank is full. Here's how to get going on the greatest trip of your life.

"I can't change."

That's the lie that keeps so many people from obeying that voice from the GUT urging change.

Of course you can change. The old idea that your character and personality are set in stone is just wrong. "Numerous studies have found evidence to the contrary," says science writer Tori Rodriguez. "New research reveals that a changing character can influence life satisfaction even more than economic upheaval."

So even more than money, or lack of it, your character is "the single biggest factor" in your happiness. We mistakenly focus on income or status—which are often hard to change—and forget that the kind of people we are makes the biggest difference to our success.[50]

No matter how old they are, most adults believe they've stopped changing and won't change much in the future. But

---

50 Rodriguez, Tori, "Life Satisfaction Linked to Personality Changes," Scientific American, July 1, 2013.

when they're asked how much they've changed in the last ten years, they report a lot of changes. It's a mistake to believe that you're going to change less than you have already changed.[51]

You're going to change a lot in the future, whether you like it or not.

The question is, will you control that change or will you just let it happen to you?

Of course you can't control everything. We all age, we're all liable to get sick or lose a job. But there is one thing we can control. The thing that matters most to our happiness, and that's our character.

This chapter is about taking off, getting started, picking up and moving, and actually making that change that will have the most impact on your future.

What is it about your character that needs to change so you can get going in life?

There are probably a lot of external things that you think are causing you to be dissatisfied or discontented with your life. Maybe it's a crummy job, or a difficult family, or an illness, or a financial setback, or a weight problem, or trouble with your friends. I can almost guarantee you that none of that matters a whole lot.

"Setbacks are no reason to jettison belief in yourself."

-Dr. Glenn Geher, State University of New York

It's your GUT that matters. As I've said before, I believe that your GUT is the voice of your character, and deep down it will tell you to get up and get going. Start that purposeful change in your life and start it now!

---

51 Miller, Greg, "Your Elusive Future Self," Science, January 3, 2013.

What do I mean by purposeful change? I mean that kind of change that makes you better—not just richer or leaner or free of any friends who are fickle. All of that is *outside* of you. I mean the kind of change that happens deep down *inside* where you live.

And the counterintuitive thing here is that if you have the GUTs to change the inside, the outside usually changes too.

I've had the experience of changing from the inside. It's tough but it's the only kind of change that matters, and the only kind that *lasts.*

During my first quarter as a Georgia Tech football player, my counselor signed me up for 20 credit hours in a variety of very hard classes. Football was a huge commitment, and I did not have any support from home. I quickly felt overwhelmed by all the class demands coupled with the physical demands on the football field and in the weight room.

I got way behind in economics and felt like I would fail the class unless I did something drastic. So I talked with some of my buddies, and we decided to cheat on the final exam—which happened to count for 75 percent of the final grade. Our group went all in for the great "cheating project." We found someone who was really smart and agreed to feed us the answers. We put a lot of time and energy into sharing those answers around. The day of the test came and I felt really confident that I was prepared to be the best cheater I could be.

Well, I took the test and later that day checked out the results. My grade was a "D." A "D"? I could have done better than that *without* cheating! I was furious. I had put all that energy into cheating and still got a crappy grade. Apparently, the teacher had staggered the tests so they all looked the same but contained slight differences—precisely in order to thwart the cheaters.

The thing is, I knew deep down that I shouldn't be cheating. My GUT had tried for weeks to get through to my head. Cheating made me feel deep down kind of sick. I had a view of myself that I couldn't succeed without cheating, but that view was all twisted up and destructive. I saw myself as inadequate to the job of succeeding with honor.

Even if I'd gotten an "A" on the test, I still would have had that nagging in the GUT. I would never get untroubled sleep, I would never trust myself totally, I would never be able to teach my own kids the importance of honesty without getting eaten up inside. Think of the kick to the GUT when you're trying hard not to be a phony, but deep down you know that you are.

So I knew I had to change. I had to stop seeing myself as inadequate, as a person who takes cheap shortcuts, a guy who just waffles his way through life by "hook or crook"—mostly crook. I knew deep down in my GUT that I was a better person than that.

My GUT taught me that it was better to learn and be curious, to ask for help when I needed it, to do my best to prepare, and then roll the dice. That day I made a GUT decision that I would never cheat again—that I would pay the price as I did in the weight room and on the football field and learn, no matter how hard the class was. Once I made that choice, my whole being felt better right down to the roots.

Well, I am pleased to say that one decision never to cheat again *in any way* changed my trajectory, my career, and my life. It was a basic change in my whole character. I graduated with honors from Georgia Tech and later graduated from a top 10 MBA program, doing quite well again. More importantly I learned how to learn, to pay the toll to gain knowledge. It has taken GUTs, and I have loved the journey the entire way.

Another major obstacle to "taking off" is "baggage."

An airplane cannot take off if it's too heavy, and a major source of weight is baggage. That's why they make you pay extra if you're carrying too much stuff with you—you'll weigh down the plane and it'll take more fuel to get off the ground.

Occasionally you see people in an airport actually throwing stuff out of their bags so they can make them lighter. Presumably they didn't need that stuff in the first place. None of it really matters a whole lot.

If you want to "take off," you'll need to lighten your load.

What bad stuff are you carrying around that is weighing you down? What can you get rid of that is keeping you from "taking off"?

It's usually resentment, bitterness, or anger over how the world has treated you. We all carry some pretty heavy baggage around. But think about it.

Mortality is a crap shoot.

There's a lot going on in the world. Great forces create unique, dynamic environments that affect billions of lives. War, terrorism, drug addiction, accidents, mental illness, abuse, and natural catastrophes—the list goes on and on. Why do so many of us suffer so much through no fault of our own? Why is there so much destruction and opposition? Who knows? But I learned very young that life was not fair.

As a father, one of my most important roles is to help my children learn how to deal with setbacks. They have heard me say so often that life isn't fair, that now they just roll their eyes and say, "Yeah, Dad, we know." So now I have a process I go through to help my kids in times of struggle.

Let's say you're going through life being good, doing your best, and working hard toward your goals—and then you get smacked really hard. Maybe, like me, your goal is to achieve great things on the football field and you get a career-ending injury. Maybe a cherished relationship goes south through no fault of yours, or you get passed over for a promotion at work in favor of someone who is clearly less qualified than you are. The scenarios are countless and very real—and often very painful. You ask, "Why me?" The very question opens the door to bitterness. "Haven't I paid the price? Aren't I worth loving? Am I too stupid to do the job? Why, why, why?" This line of logic is just hurtful and keeps getting worse the more you dwell on it.

So this is what I tell my kids (and myself) when facing setbacks:

We all carry a garbage bag through life. We put all the bad things that happen to us into the bag. Over time the bag gets heavier and heavier. When we feel sorry for ourselves, we open the bag and start digging around in it. "Remember when so-and-so did such-and-such to you? Remember when you failed that test even after you studied like crazy? Remember when you worked your heart out on that job and they fired you anyway? Remember when you ran for class office and lost the election to the biggest jerk in school?" It fills your heart with anger. Bitter feelings ooze through your veins like poison from a venomous snake bite. You get more and more worked up, cankered, and nasty because life is *simply not fair!*

But the moment you open up your bag of crap and stir it up, you produce nothing but stink. My advice to you is to throw the damn bag away. Forgive the people who have harmed you. Let things go. Correct your course if you can so it won't happen again. Learn from the experience.

After you throw the bag away, listen to your GUT. *It will tell you that the bad things that happen to you can actually be good for you.* I know that sounds crazy, but it's true. If you fail a test, you might see it as an opportunity to expand your understanding so you don't fail the next time. If you lose a job, you might see it as a chance to create the job you really wanted all along. (If, as in my case, one career ends because of an injury, you can find a fulfilling career that won't wreck your body!)

"I don't believe in a lot of baggage. It's such a nuisance. Life's too short to fuss with it."

–Dr. Doolittle

Even if you can't recover what you've lost in a terrible setback, you still gain. What you gain are the gifts that are only meaningful deep down inside of you—gifts like humility, patience, endurance, resilience, and most of all, compassion.

I believe compassion is what makes us human. Compassion always makes things better. The compassion you gain from your own suffering can help others in unfathomable ways. For example, suppose a close friend experiences a death in the family. What do you do? Nothing you do or say can bring the loved one back, but you can show compassion. You can love them, be close, say nothing, maybe cry with them, and let them know they are not alone in their darkest hour. Down deep in your GUT, you will know what to do because you know how it feels to hurt terribly.

So get rid of the garbage bag and pack a different bag. Maybe it's an orange duffel bag like mine, or a yellow backpack or a purple purse. But pack that bag with these things:

- Lessons learned from setbacks;

- Renewed vision, hopes, and dreams;

- Love and kindness;

- Humility, patience, endurance, resilience;

- And compassion

Not surprisingly, that bag is much lighter and smells way better. Inside that bag are the tools that enable you to build the life you *really* want deep down in your GUT. And in the end, you will be very grateful for this bag—grateful for the good stuff *and* the bad, for the victories *and* the challenges.

The worst of things can be the best of things. The harder things get, the better you get. The worse the odds, the greater the triumph in the end. If you had tried to tell me that when I was suffering through my whacked-out childhood, I would have asked you what you were smoking. But it's true! I have told my own painful story to thousands of people with no other motive

The Fox and the Cat

A Fox was boasting to a Cat of its clever devices for escaping its enemies.

"I have a whole bag of tricks," he said, *"which contains a hundred ways of escaping my enemies."*

"I have only one," said the Cat; *"but I can generally manage with that."*

Just at that moment they heard the cry of a pack of hounds coming towards them, and the Cat immediately scampered up a tree and hid herself in the boughs.

"This is my plan," said the Cat. *"What are you going to do?"*

The Fox thought first of one way, then of another, and while he was debating the hounds came nearer and nearer, and at last the Fox in his confusion was caught up by the hounds and soon killed by the huntsmen.

The Moral of the Story: Too much information can be dangerous.

From Aesop's Fables

than to give them courage and hope. The funny thing is that doing so has blessed my life beyond measure.

So when people whine to me about how unfair their lives are and how much they suffer and how everything sucks, I ask, "What is that smell?"

Now, in order to change, you have to decide to change. You just have to. Your GUT is telling you to change, but how do you start? How do you actually *take off*?

No airline pilot takes off without preparation. She goes through a standard checklist to make sure everything is in working order. She has a flight plan in front of her. She has a support team in the plane and on the ground.

Nobody climbs into the cockpit without any training or preparation expecting to fly the plane. But we do similar things all the time when we try to change our lives. Only an idiot gets up one morning and decides to do strenuous exercise. He'll kill himself. He'll get injured and fall apart and then there's no exercise program. Some people go on crash diets and then they crash—which is a word your airline pilot doesn't want to hear. You've got to get educated and prepared before you make a major change in your life.

But don't make the mistake the procrastinating professor made. He spent years studying and even teaching exercise science but never did much exercising himself. His excuse was that he hadn't learned enough about it yet to commit himself to a particular program. Eventually his health collapsed.

This is another mistake we make: "I'm not sure." "I don't know if I can commit yet." "It's a big commitment—maybe I should think about it some more." These are the people who never get their college diplomas, who never go for the job they really want, who bypass good relationships and good times because they're "just not sure yet." Of course we need good information, but as the pilot knows, at some point the plane has to take off.

One new problem we have today is *too much* information. We can get so overwhelmed with data that we are paralyzed. That's when we need to listen to the GUT. As John Naisbitt, the author of *Megatrends*, says, "Intuition becomes increasingly valuable in the new information society precisely because there is so much data."

Jeni Britton Bauer had an idea for a new business. It would be a different kind of business, focused on making the absolute best product in the world while employing people who really need jobs—the poor and the disabled—and providing opportunities for such people to own their own "scoop shops" around the U.S.A. Now, starting a business is a high risk most people don't want to take, but Jeni has followed her GUT to great success with Jeni's Splendid Ice Creams.

Of course Jeni puts a lot of effort into research. But she says, "It's about making a decision, sticking with it, and learning from it. With my ice cream flavors, even when I'm not sure people will like them, if my team does, I go with my GUT and release them. You learn from mistakes, and then your GUT is more educated. Especially starting a business, if you think too much, you'll never do it. Research is good, but eventually knowledge can become paralyzing. Turn off your brain and jump off the cliff. You can build the parachute on the way down." [52]

Let's look closely at what Jeni is saying. Even with good preparation, there comes that time when you've got to start the change. You don't know if it's going to work out, but if you stick with it you'll learn, and by learning you'll get better.

Educating the GUT is a powerful concept we will talk more about later. But for now, remember the pattern here: Do your homework, then "go with the GUT and release"! There is such a thing as too little preparation, but it's just as bad to put off change all of your life because you're never "ready." If you're reasonably prepared, there comes a point where you have to "turn off your brain and jump off the cliff."

When you jump, you won't land perfectly, so don't expect it. According to psychologists, "One of life's sharpest paradoxes is that the key to satisfaction is doing things that feel risky, uncomfortable, and occasionally bad. . . . Too much focus on minutiae can be exhausting and paralyzing. The happiest among us cheerfully accept that striving for perfection—and a perfectly smooth interaction with everyone at all times—is a loser's bet." [53]

You're the creator of your own character. You're the pilot of your own life. Isn't it time for you to "take off"?

52 Cited in Webber, Rebecca, "5 Times to Go With Your GUT," RealSimple.com, http://www.realsimple.com/work-life/life-strategies/GUT-instinct.

53 Biswas-Diener, Robert and Todd B. Kashdan, "What Happy People Do Differently," Psychology Today, July 2, 2013.

Go With Your GUT!

Answer these questions for yourself. Write down your answers.

1. If you already know you want to change, what's keeping you from "taking off?"

2. When have you taken a big risk and failed? What did you learn? When have you taken a big risk and succeeded? What did you learn?

3. If you're dissatisfied with your life in any way, have you considered that it might be something in your character that needs to change? Or are you too focused on changing your circumstances?

4. Are you waiting for circumstances to be just right before you go for the change you know you want to make? Are you forever "getting ready" to make those vital changes? Isn't time to "take off?"

CHAPTER 9

Paying the Price

Be glad for the hard things. Hard work doesn't make you weary—the "fog" makes you weary. The fog sets in when you can't see in front of you why the hard work is necessary. Fatigue is more an emotional state than a physical state. Too many of us "suffer" with pain—instead, we should enjoy all the throbbing, smarting, stinging, and aching that go along with "GUTting it out"

"It's too hard."

That's another great lie that keeps so many people from obeying that voice from the GUT that urges change.

Whether you're a nine-year-old whining because you have to practice the piano or a 20-year-old facing years of college or a 50-year-old trying to get back in shape, it's all "too hard."

But how does that work for you?

I have learned to rejoice when things are hard. I love it when there's something so important to me that I'm willing to hurt for it. I know it makes no sense and it's totally counterintuitive, but when your purpose and vision are big enough, even the pain of getting there is pleasure.

| GUTS

This chapter is about paying the price to achieve your vision. It's about "GUTting it out." It's also about the joy and satisfaction that come from paying the price.

Why do you feel better after exercising? Even if your feet hurt and your muscles ache, you feel better. After lifting weights I often think "I feel really good!" Of course doctors will tell you that while you exercise the brain releases endorphins to help you minimize stress and pain. True, but I also feel satisfied with myself, deep down satisfied, because I know I've done something good for myself. It's my GUT rejoicing. When I lie around doing nothing and avoid exercise, my GUT hurts me in a bad way. It nags at me, badgering, pestering, and harassing me until I get up and do something good for myself.

My friend Sean was a college quarterback. He told me how there were days on the practice field when one guy would start to slack off just a little in giving his best effort, then another guy would do the same, and pretty soon the whole group was running just a little below top speed or doing just a little less than they could. Usually the coaches wouldn't even recognize what was going on. Sean calls it "social loafing."

But, he says, once in a while one player wouldn't join in the social loafing. He'd sprint as fast as he could and leave everyone else in the dust.

Why do we loaf around and refuse to do the hard things? Down in the GUT we know the hard things are the best things. The GUT tells us in plain terms that if we're not the one sprinting as hard and fast as we can, we're going to be unhappy with ourselves. And that feels lousy. It feels a lot worse to do the easy things than it does to do the hard things.

It just does. Your GUT knows it and you know it.

"But, Sam," I hear you saying, "you're just crazy. Life is already hard enough without trying to make it harder. You talk about running even harder and faster? I get tired just thinking about it."

Okay, here's a surprise for you. The reason you're tired is that you're *not* running as fast as you can.

If you've ever been in a race or just watched one, you know that everything speeds up just at the last moment. There's a burst of effort that arises out of nowhere. The runners suddenly explode with energy. Even at the end of a 26-mile marathon when the racers look like zombies ready to disintegrate on the track, there's an abrupt shot at the finish line.

Here they are, totally out of breath, near dropping with exhaustion, but all at once racing like the wind for the finish. What happened?

"Fatigue, discomfort, discouragement are just symptoms of effort."

–Morgan Freeman, actor

Dr. Timothy David Noakes, one of the world's great exercise scientists, has thought about this a lot. "In the case of a close finish, physiology does not determine who wins. Rather somewhere in the final section of the race, the brains of the second, and lower placed finishers, accept their respective finishing positions and no longer challenge for a higher finish. The winner's brain simply doesn't give in."

In other words, the winner decides to win, while the losers are just "tired."

Dr. Noakes goes on to say, "Sensations of fatigue are . . . illusionary since their generation is largely independent of the real biological state of the athlete at the time they develop." This means that fatigue is an illusion. Fatigue is not in your body—it's in your head.

As a kid I loved to run. One Saturday afternoon when I was nine years old, my stepfather told me to grab my sneakers and put on some shorts and a t-shirt. I ask why and he said we going to the AAU junior Olympics at the University of Nevada-Las Vegas, and he was going to enter me. Sounded fine.

The next thing I knew I was throwing the shotput farther than anyone. I was tall for my age—over 5 feet and weighed over 130 pounds—big for a nine-year-old. Then he put me in the 880-yard race—twice around the track. I lined up with a lot of very tiny kids. I must have outweighed the biggest of them by at least 50 pounds. The gun went off and we scrambled to take our place. The first lap was hard but I managed to stay near the front of the pack. It looked ridiculous to see this portly Clydesdale type of kid bounding along amidst all the skinny thoroughbreds. It was all I could do to just keep up.

I managed to stay near the front well into the second lap. With a hundred yards to go, something happened I can't explain to this day. Literally dying on the vine with nothing in the tank to finish the last 100 yards, I saw out of the corner of my eye my stepfather and little brother screaming, "Go! Go! Go! Right now, Sammy! Kick it! Take it!" It felt like a thunder clap. My body filled with instant energy and I started to sprint. First passing one kid, then another, I soon had the leader in sight; and with just 10 yards left, I gave everything I had inside of me. I drew from deep inside my GUT. I decided that I was going to win this damn race.

I crossed the finish line and immediately collapsed on the track.

My dad and brother came screaming over to me. "Sammy, you won, you got a gold medal." Then the official came by and said, "Son, you just broke a state record in your age group for the 880." I was just amazed. What were the odds? Here I was fat, out of shape, and wearing crappy gear—and I took State. That day I came home with three gold medals and renewed confidence in myself because I had found it in my GUT to win.

The power was there all the time. My head was telling me, "It's time to die on the vine, to give up, to stop trying so hard. You're exhausted. You're out of energy." But my GUT was sending me a different message: "It's time to kick it! It's time to win! You'll love it!"

Where did that last spurt of energy come from? Of course the body undergoes changes when we're exercising hard, and naturally we think we're getting tired. But Dr. Noakes is fascinated by that "end spurt" when supposedly we're too tired to go on.

He asks, "Exactly what is fatigue?" Is it that your muscles slow down and can't do any more? "According to this definition, the athlete who speeds up near the end of exercise cannot be fatigued, regardless of how she feels." Dr. Noakes explains that at no time when person in good health is exercising does he or she even get close to the point where they can't do more.[54]

Legendary football coach Vince Lombardi used to say, "Fatigue makes us all cowards." Actually, he got it exactly backwards: Fear, holding back, "social loafing"—these are the things that produce fatigue.

The way I figure it, you pay a price whether you go for your best or you settle for less. The price you pay for settling is disappointment in yourself that will linger in your GUT. It's a pain called low self-esteem, and it's located in your abdomen. I've felt it, and you've felt it.

Doing a lot of busy but relatively meaningless work produces a "fog" in my mind. Does the same thing happen to you? My whole life turns fuzzy. I can't remember one day from the next.

If you've ever walked or driven a car in the fog you know what I mean. Your eyes are on the ground because you can't see ahead of you; and if you try, it's just frustrating. You take little steps or drive very slowly because you can't tell where you are, where you've been, or where you're going.

---

54 Noakes, Timothy David, "Fatigue is a brain-derived emotion that regulates the exercise behavior to ensure the protection of whole body homeostasis." Frontiers in Physiology, April 11, 2012. http://dx.doi.org/10.3389/fphys.2012.00082

"Brain fog includes symptoms of confusion, forgetfulness, and lack of focus and mental clarity. . . . It means there's an imbalance in your life that needs to be addressed."

–Deane Alban, writer on brain science

The same thing happens if we're not listening to the GUT. The GUT tells us where to go and what to do. If you get to the point where you really know how to listen, it will guide pretty much every step you take. But if days turn into weeks and months where you're not listening to that voice inside you that gives you direction, you'll find yourself continually disoriented and exhausted.

So when you say you're too tired, fine. Get some sleep and then listen to your GUT. Get up and get going. But if you're always whining about how tired you are—how beat and bushed and pooped and drained and wearied and worn out you are—it's likely that you're not listening to your GUT. Unless you've got a health problem that produces fatigue, you're avoiding the hard joys of life.

One way I can tell if you're listening to your GUT is to ask you how tired you are. Almost everybody will say, "I'm so exhausted," but then I watch them. If they're deep down excited about what they're doing, they *never* get tired of it. They might say they're tired, but they're not. Just watch. The people who don't get tired are the ones who are listening to the GUT because, as I said in the first chapter, they're doing what they were *born to do*!

Of course they need sleep like anyone else, but they can go hard at it all day without even noticing time passing or energy draining. They are paying the price, all right, but they have an inexhaustible wealth of energy.

That's what I mean by "GUTting it out." I don't mean that you should suffer pointlessly and just "endure" life and show a lot of grit. For me "GUTting it out" means calling on all that bottomless energy you have for doing what matters most to you.

Then there's the opposite kind of people—the ones who never seem to have any energy and drain the energy out of everyone else around them.

Have you ever noticed that some people seem to enjoy talking about how tired they are and how painful their lives are? They're called "martyrs." They like the sympathy they get when they talk about how hard everything is for them. They call attention to their pain and use it to get their way or to manipulate other people. These professional victims get a lot of mileage out of their pain. Even though they complain that the price of change is so painful, they never really pay that price because it's too profitable for them not to.

The truth is, you can choose how you will deal with pain the same way you can choose every other response to life.

Take weight lifting, an exercise I have come to love. You can't change the fact that lactic acid builds up in your muscles when you put them under stress, and that the result is pain that grows and grows. But you can choose how to deal with that fact. You can complain, avoid, procrastinate, grumble about how unfair it is, and give a half-hearted effort. Or you can do the opposite: attack the weights, have fun, laugh, sweat, and "feel the burn"—and you'll get stronger. In my experience, you'll feel better in every way. Your head tells you you've done something to strengthen your body, and your GUT congratulates you on doing what you know deep down you *should* do.

My experience tells me that pain can be pleasure. I know it sounds crazy, but it's true.

There are two definitions of pleasure: (1) a feeling of happy satisfaction and enjoyment, and (2) sensual gratification. For me, #2 is actually a counterfeit. Why? Because living for sensual gratification is purposeless and in the end not a pleasure at all.

A life of purpose is a true pleasure. A life driven by hard, meaningful work is a pleasure.

The Joy of Doing Hard Things

Running a marathon is one of the hardest things human beings do. The 26-mile race takes endurance, determination, and GUTs. To a lot of us, it sounds awfully painful, and we're programmed to avoid pain, right? So why do people do it?

The answer seems to be, for the joy of it. Many marathon runners describe a strange kind of overwhelming delight they feel after they've been running for a while. Some call it "flow," others call it "the zone" or "runner's high." In French it's called la *volupté*, a feeling of total sensuous well-being.

One Kenyan marathon runner calls it "Spirit." He says he endures 125 miles of running a week just so he can feel this pure, sweet happiness. "The harder you train, the more you get the Spirit," he says. "It gains on you."

Ed Caesar, Two Hours: The Quest to Run the Impossible Marathon, Viking, 2015, 4.

A life of aimless, counterfeit "pleasure," on the other hand, produces shame and *self-disgust*, an emotion that you feel deep down in your GUT.

Please don't get me wrong. Loafing is sometimes the best thing for you. So veg out once in a while with a movie or skip an occasional workout to catch a dumb TV show. But as psychologists Robert Biswas-Diener and Todd Kashdan tell us, "If you're primarily focused on activities that feel good in the moment, you may miss out on the benefits of developing a clear purpose. Purpose is what drives us to take risks and make changes—even in the face of hardship. . . . Overall, people who are the happiest tend to be superior at sacrificing short-term pleasures when there is a good opportunity to make progress toward what they aspire to become in life." [55] A life without fun is no fun. Of course. But I have to ask, what is "fun"? I know people who live to go to the amusement park every single weekend. I know people who get drunk every night. I know people who get home from work and collapse in front of the TV or bury themselves in social media till 4 in the morning.

Is that fun?

55 Biswas-Diener, Robert and Todd B. Kashdan, "What Happy People Do Differently," Psychology Today, July 2, 2013.

For me, a little of that sort of fun goes a long way. After a while my GUT says, "That's enough. I've had it with that kind of fun. Now let's go have some real fun."

And what my GUT means by that is that it's time to get to work on what really matters to me. It's time to "GUT it out," to do the hard things that, for me, are the real pleasure in life—writing to help others, giving speeches to lift others, teaching classes to encourage others, and most of all giving my best effort to my family.

I've learned that giving too much time to aimless fun actually gives me a stomach ache. My GUT rebels at it. Pretty soon that ache turns into a spiritual ache, a longing to be doing what matters.

I once attended a seminar on negotiation where they tried to teach us to cut corners and lie and fake out the other party. I couldn't believe what I was hearing, but other people in the room were lapping it up. The teacher kept telling us about how fun it is to take advantage of people and stay on top and to "win, win, win." She made sure we understood that people are either winners or losers, and we didn't want to be losers.

At one point I turned to my friend who attended the seminar with me and I said, "I'm in hell." My GUT was literally twisting up inside of me. He felt the same way. We both went away from the seminar feeling serious pain—physical and spiritual pain. We were both very glad to get away from that destructive, counterfeit notion of "fun."

Unfortunately, lots of people get a lot of "pleasure" out of cheating, loafing, and playing the victim. But in the end their pleasure is just empty, and it often leads to the kind of pain that really hurts—mental anguish.

In Shakespeare's play *Henry V*, the king of England talks about how jealous he is of the common people who don't have to deal with all the violence and corruption of politics. He thinks how wonderful it would be to put in a day's "profitable labor" and then go to bed and "sleep in Elysium," another word for heavenly peace. Hard work is the price you pay for peaceful sleep, and nothing in this world is better than earning some peaceful sleep.

| GUTS

You can't sleep if your GUT is churning all the time. Your GUT won't let you sleep unless you put in a day's hard, worthwhile, meaningful work.

So when you start thinking "It's too hard," remember that's a big lie. If you catch yourself whimpering about how hard it is to make a meaningful life, just remember that it's a lot harder *not* to live a meaningful life.

When you start whining and feeling sorry for yourself because it's all "too hard," listen to your GUT. It will tell you to get up, to push on, and to keep going. It will tell you that the real fun is in doing the hard things. It will tell you that you'll feel disgusted with yourself if you don't do the hard things.

I have a good friend who loves playing the piano. He's not a pro or anything like that, but he just loves making music. It wasn't always so. As a child he hated practicing. As a teenager he loafed, but he never stopped loving the music. In the end he "GUTted it out"—he paid the price to become pretty good at it, but it was the hardest thing he's ever done. He says that whenever he sees a piano now, his heart pounds to play it. He looks at new pieces with excitement, wondering if he can conquer them.

"It's the hard pieces that are the most fun," he says. "Easy stuff doesn't give a lot of satisfaction. But when you really master a piece by Chopin or Rachmaninoff, you get this deep, deep pride that wells up inside of you."

Now, my friend doesn't play for money. It's not his profession. But it means a lot to him to be able to do it well and do it gracefully. He does it for himself—to challenge himself to "GUT it out," to do the really hard thing with joy and relish and to conquer it.

He calls that fun. And so do I.

Go With Your GUT!

Answer these questions for yourself. Write down your answers.

1. When have you backed away from doing hard things that would make your life more meaningful? How do you feel about those things now?

2. Do you feel tired all the time? Do you complain about being too busy and constantly exhausted? Ask yourself deep down—are the things you're so busy doing really worthwhile? Do you complain about being tired in order to be a bit of a "martyr"? What is your GUT telling you?

3. Are there changes you really ought to make in your life but you've hesitated because it would be "too hard" to make them?

4. What price do you need to pay in order to become the person you really want to be? Are you willing to pay that price?

CHAPTER 10

Winning Every Step of the Way

Winning Every Step of the Way

The most successful people win consistently and often. Does that mean they don't fail? Not at all—and here's the counterintuitive thing about failure. To fail is to win. Yes, that's right. You can't win unless you fail and "push past failure:" That's what "GUTting it out" means.

"I don't want to try. I know I'll just fail."

Of course you will.

You will fail many, many times as you try to change.

And I'm not just going to toss out the old saying that "it's only a failure if you don't try again." Although that principle is true enough, that's not what I'm talking about.

I'm saying that failure is *necessary* to winning.

Here's what I mean.

Suppose you're trying to build strength by weight lifting. The real benefit of weight training is to work to failure. Then the real

145

Famous Failures

Arguably the world's most famous chef, Julia Child failed the final exam at the world-renowned Cordon Bleu cooking school the first time she took it. She demanded a second chance and passed.

Walt Disney's first cartoon company, Laugh-o-Gram, went bankrupt in 1922.

In 1947, Twentieth-Century Fox passed on hiring Marilyn Monroe because, they told her, she wasn't pretty and couldn't act.

J.K. Rowling's first book was rejected by eight (that's 8!) publishers before a little company called Bloomsbury picked it up. Its title: *Harry Potter and the Sorcerer's Stone*.

Michael Jordan, who many say is the greatest basketball player of all time, was cut from his high school team.

"I have missed more than 9,000 shots in my career. I have lost almost 300 games. On 26 occasions I have been entrusted to take the game winning shot, and I missed. I have failed over and over and over again in my life. And that is why I succeed."

–*Michael Jordan*

gains begin. That's right—in the weight room you don't win unless you lift weights to the point where your muscles literally fail you.

It's all in the science. In one classic study, 26 elite college athletes were divided into two groups. Both groups did bench presses three times a week for six weeks. One group was asked to lift weights to the point where they couldn't lift any more—in other words, to failure. The other group was asked to lift the same number of times but in shorter sets with lighter weights, that is, not to failure.

At the end of six weeks the failure group was 10 percent stronger and 10 percent more powerful.[56] The other group was only about 5 percent stronger and 6 percent more powerful. In other words, by *failing* you can get twice as strong and nearly twice as powerful as you can without failing.

Why is this so?

When exercised, your muscles "fail" at the point when they can no longer produce enough force to overcome the load. Remember this: the

---

56 Willardson, J.M. (2007). The application of training to failure in periodized multiple-set resistance exercise programs. Journal of Strength and Conditioning Research. 21(2), 628-631.

muscle fibers aren't entirely fatigued at this point, they just can't produce enough force to lift that load.

But it's the failure that builds the muscle. "When muscles are overloaded during weight lifting, little tears are made in the muscle itself," explains Michael Moses, team doctor for the U.S. Marines Marathon. "This micro trauma may sound harmful but is in fact the natural response of your muscles. . . . The muscle repairs these tears when you're resting, and this helps muscles grow in size and strength." [57]

The muscles are actually injured, torn up, and exhausted in the process of weight lifting. The muscle gets to a point where it just gives up—can't do any more—sorry. That's it. I'm beaten. I've had it. I'm done.

And that, my friends, is *failure*.

"The bottom line: training to failure is more important than the load, per se. In order to increase muscle mass and get stronger, train to failure."

—**Sports Illustrated** [58]

But here's the miracle: That poor failed muscle goes to work repairing itself, restoring injured tissue so it can handle heavier loads next time. The cells of the muscle become stronger. The chemistry of the muscle "learns" how to handle an increased load. The outcome: a bigger and better muscle.

Ironically, the muscle cannot succeed unless it fails first!

---

57 Cited in Carpenter, Leanna, "How Muscles Get Big," Weightwatchers.com. http://www.weightwatchers.com/util/art/index_art.aspx?tabnum=1&art_id=60361&sc=3405

58 Joyner, Michael J. "Training to Failure: Myth or Method to Muscle Mass and Strength Gains?" Sports Illustrated, July 11, 2016. http://www.si.com/edge/2016/07/11/training-failure-muscle-mass-strength-gains

This is the basic principle of resistance training, and it is *a basic principle of life.*

Please don't misunderstand me. Failure can be the result of poor preparation, out-of-control behavior, or bad motives. I'm not talking about that kind of failure—the catastrophic failed life of a drug addict or a cheat or a person who can't control his anger.

Note that weight lifting is "controlled" failure. You don't just walk into the gym and try to squat lift 400 pounds the first day. You'll wreck your back and end up in the hospital. That is an uncontrolled failure.

"Controlled failure" is what happens when a wise person pushes herself in a measured, careful way to the failure point. When she prepares thoughtfully, takes a meaningful risk, and pushes herself up to her limits. If she doesn't test her limits, she doesn't grow.

Most people who start lifting weights rarely pay the price to get past the sourness and muscle pain of failure to find the real joy in lifting. I learned early the joy of lifting and quickly moved past the initial pain and difficulty by lifting often with great intensity, because I wanted the benefits of being stronger, bigger, and faster for football. As a kid moving in and out of poverty and abuse, every extra moment I could spend in the gym or weight room brought me sheer happiness and joy. I just loved it, even though it was very difficult. The key was the "why": I lifted to become a great football player and athlete, and in the process got hooked on the joy of pushing and pulling volumes of weight and the benefits it brought to me physically.

Of course my muscles failed. They failed every day. They were *supposed* to fail—in a controlled way. But each failure brought me closer to fulfilling my purpose. This is why I say that even though I was failing a lot, I was *winning every step of the way*.

"GUTting it out" means winning every step of the way. "GUTting it out" also means failing consistently. "GUTting it out" is failing so you *can* succeed. That takes GUTs!

Every failure tears you up. It exhausts you. It leaves you busted and broken and played out. It's supposed to. There is no other way to really learn and grow than by pushing yourself hard to the failure point.

When I began to understand this principle, I found I could apply the lessons from the weight room to other areas of my life. Learning and literacy for instance. I love to read, learn, and ask questions every day. I am naturally curious and constantly try to gain knowledge and wisdom. I am constantly failing at understanding the things I read, but I find that pondering and going back and trying again is the key. Sometimes I ask stupid questions and look silly, but the benefit of learning far outweighs the drawbacks of looking awkward.

My wife is an amazing musician and has the voice of an angel. Years ago after she completed her fifth album, I got the bright idea to take guitar lessons. I thought it would be awesome to be able to accompany Ms. Kim's bright, beautiful folk sound during family gatherings and events. So for my birthday Kim bought me a *killer* limited edition Ovation electric acoustic guitar with wild red flames painted on the body.

I started playing the guitar with great excitement, learning blues riffs and folk tunes and all. But in the initial phases of learning, my fingers would get so sore I could not feel them anymore. I would practice and my fingers would hurt for days, so I would stop practicing until they felt better. That's how it works, just as in weight lifting. I knew that. I also knew that eventually callouses would form and my fingers would grow strong enough to get past the hurt.

The problem was not that I never succeeded, but that I quit failing. I never practiced long enough for those callouses to develop so I could move past the pain and make real gains and get the real benefit of being able to play. I did not have the love or longing to be good enough to experience the joy on the other side of the pain. I did not have the GUTs to learn the guitar.

Don't Give Up— Change Takes Time

Don't buy into any promise of "instant, radical change" in your life.

At Michigan State and University of Illinois, researchers asked a group of students to set concrete goals for changing their character (like becoming more extraverted or more emotionally stable).

Over a 16-week semester, the students did show growth in the direction they wanted, but the changes were "middling."

The lesson? Adopt goals that are achievable. Fad diets, instant makeovers, and so forth *just don't work.*

It usually takes years to develop new habits, so be patient with yourself.

Deep down in your GUT, you know this.

Scott Barry Kaufman, "Can Personality Be Changed?" The Atlantic, July 26, 2016.

I still hold on to that guitar in hopes that one day I will someday have the GUTs to learn how to play the guitar and perform with Kim and my other family members.

Are you afraid of failure? Remember Jeni of Jeni's Splendid Ice Creams? "Failure is the way we learn."

"True champions aren't always the ones that win, but those with the most GUTs."

– Mia Hamm, two-time Olympic gold medal soccer player

Are you afraid of failure? Remember Shakespeare: "Our doubts are traitors, and make us lose the good we oft might win, by fearing to attempt."

Are you afraid of failure? Remember J.K. Rowling, the author of the blockbuster Harry Potter series who went from being homeless to being one of the most successful writers in the world: "Failure is so important. We speak about success all the time. It is the ability to use failure that often leads to greater success. I've met people who don't want to try for fear of failing."

Failure is so important. I love that observation.

One of the ways I dealt with the stresses and challenges of an abusive home growing up was playing football. It just seemed natural for me. I sort of loved knocking the crap out of people, taking all my life's frustrations out on the opposing team's players and getting positive reinforcement for it. Out of all the things I could be good at, my GUT told me that my best avenue to a great future was through football. I was big for my age, fairly fast, and I could hit people very hard.

At times I found myself homeless in high school, bouncing from place to place, keeping my troubles a secret because of the shame of my circumstances. Regardless of where I was staying, I usually got to school early, studied, lifted weights and worked out like crazy, coming home late every day, all to reach my goal to be the best football player I could become, get a college scholarship, and be able to play in the pros.

The funny thing? The hard work was an absolute joy. I loved lifting weights, running sprints, practicing, and doing skill work. I worked harder than anyone on my team. They did not seem to want to work as hard as I did and did not get the same reward I did from hard work. It was in my GUT. I couldn't rest if I wasn't working hard, and as a result I was recruited to play ball by schools all over the country. I landed a full-ride scholarship to that great football school, Georgia Tech.

This was a very big deal to me and to folks who knew me. When I left Las Vegas at 18 years old I had been homeless for almost three years, and everything I owned in the world fit into an old orange duffel bag I got at football camp when I was 14 years old. As I arrived in Atlanta, Georgia, with my duffel bag full of hopes and dreams, I immediately went to work. This time it was a bit harder to separate myself from the other players. They worked hard too, and they had a lot of God-given talent.

My freshman year I excelled in school and sports. I played a lot as a freshman in big games in front of thousands of people. My hard work had paid off. At the end of my freshman year I was in a position to start as a sophomore, and I was named to the

All ACC Freshman Newcomers Team (sort of a freshman all-star team). I was a dean's list student, and things were going well. I was well on my way to playing in the pros. In my annual review meeting with Coach Bill Curry, he suggested that if things continued the way they were going, I had a chance to become an All American and a top round pick in the NFL draft. My hard work was continuing to pay off.

Six months later my career was over. I blew out both of my shoulders during spring football practice. I was devastated. My entire self-worth was connected to my performance on the football field. As I met with our team doctor, Fred Allman, he delivered the bad news. "Sam, both your shoulders have been permanently damaged, and I think your career is finished."

"No Doc, it can't be, I just got to play ball. I will do anything, just give me a fighting chance to come back and play." Dr. Allman then suggested I have some significant, radical reconstructive surgeries that might give me a chance to play again. "It will be difficult, but I think it just might work," he said. Before I left his office I had both surgeries scheduled six weeks apart. There had to be a way to accomplish my goals.

I woke up from surgery, tubes everywhere, projectile vomiting, screaming, absolutely terrified. "What did they do to me?" Dr. Allman explained in gruesome detail all the things they did to stabilize my shoulder. He told me that I had to keep my shoulder completely immobilized for six weeks or it would ruin the surgery and we would have to start over. Even now the odds were totally against my ever returning to the team.

After six weeks, when I could barely move my right shoulder, I had my left shoulder operated on. I woke from that surgery with the same tubes coming out of my shoulders, screaming in pain and vomiting everywhere, asking the same question, "What did they do to me?" "The same thing, genius." Then through physical therapy I began to regain the flexibility and muscle mass I had lost. It was excruciating. What a nightmare that was.

I worked hard for months and seemed to be making no progress. What the hell was up with that? I thought. I had been taught my entire life that hard work always pays off. That you had to GUT it out if you wanted to reach your goals. But this time it was different. I sank deep into depression. All those years, all that work, for nothing. Doubt filled my soul.

Then my friends, who knew me as a happy-go-lucky, hard-working kid, noticed my fallen state. They approached me. "Bracken, we know what you need—a road trip." This was code for, "we need a designated driver to take us to Florida over spring break." So they convinced me to pile into my friend Andy's van—all thirteen of us—and I drove to Florida for spring break. We arrived at this beautiful resort. Two guys got one room where all 13 of us stayed—sort of the college economies of scale—but we did not care about the room, we cared about all the fine-looking women we wanted to have a good time with.

It was a beach front resort with an awesome pool area right on the Atlantic Ocean. The view was absolutely spectacular, clear coastal blue water, wonderful temperature, and beautiful women everywhere. The scene could not have been more perfect for my buddies. I, on the other hand, was in complete and utter hell. In a lounge chair in the dirt beside the pool, I sat the entire day witnessing all my teammates having the time of their lives, frolicking with all these fine-looking co-eds.

As the day went on, they had more and more fun and I sank deeper and deeper into hell. I was in a lot of pain and not particularly in a party mood. The tide came in and then went out—as it withdrew, it was like it took all my hope with it. "There it goes," I said. "My life sucks, and it can't get much worse than it is right here, right now." And at that very moment a flock of seagulls flew right over me, and, yes, they did—they crapped all over me. My friends looked at me and exploded laughing. "Bracken, you look like a crapping stick." Ha, ha.

At that very moment, I was taught one of life's most valuable lessons. Deep down, my GUT told me that if I went around

153

feeling sorry for myself—"Woe is me, I'm a homeless abused kid and my football career is over and I'm a big failure and I'm good for nothing but to have birds crap on me"—I would forever *be* a crapping stick. I would *become* a failure. That moment became a defining moment. The odds began to turn in my favor.

I listened to my GUT. I returned to Atlanta with a new commitment. Yes, I had failed, but I was not a failure. I started getting up at 4:30 a.m. and ran across campus to the student center and swam in an Olympic-size pool for one hour. Then I ran back across campus and climbed the fence at Bobby Dodd stadium and ran all of the stadium stairs—that took another hour. Before my teammates were getting out of bed for breakfast, I had worked out for two-and-a-half hours. Then I went to class. After class I went to physical therapy, then to the weight room, then to calculus tutoring—and I rinsed and repeated for months. I started to feel joyful again and full of hope that my hard work would pay off.

But again, I was making few gains. It was like I was working and working but not getting anywhere.

So I visited Coach Curry and explained my frustration. "Coach, I want so badly to come back from the surgeries, earn a starting position, make great contributions to our team, and get my chance to play pro ball. But for the first time in my life, my hard work is not working."

Coach Curry, a man of great love and wisdom, saw in me something I did not see in myself. I'm sure he had a GUT feeling about me. He saw more than just a football player. He saw a whole person with unlimited potential and unique gifts to give the world. He listened to me and then smiled and suggested that I do the following:

1. Go to the bookstore and get a three-ring binder.

2. Get 4 tabs and label them Mind, Body, Heart, and Soul.

3. Put blank paper behind each tab.

4. Then behind each tab write down a personal inventory—take a cold hard look in the mirror—evaluate where you are right now in your life. Be honest with yourself.

5. Then behind each tab, write down where you want to be one year from now – make sure you pick just one goal for each of the four areas, a big goal that really stretches you. Get really clear on what you want to accomplish – the clearer you are, the greater chance you have of accomplishing the goal.

6. After that turn the page and write down "new and better" behavior that you need to do to accomplish the goal. What is your GUT telling you?

7. Finally, turn the page and write down a compelling reason for accomplishing the goal. Remember, there is great power in purpose.

8. Open that book and review it every day. After three weeks, tear out the section on where you are right now. Then think through what you are doing, why you're doing it and how to do it every day. Chunk things down, follow your GUT, and understand I am here for you if you need anything.

I thought, "What do I have to lose?" I read that goal book every day. I focused on where I was going, why I was going there, and how I was going to get there. And it changed everything. I put four crazy big goals in that book:

1. Gain a starting position—be "All Conference."

2. Raise my GPA so I can graduate with honors.

3. Dramatically improve my family relationships and gain new friends.

4. Grow spiritually and be more centered.

Now this is the thing.

I had been running and swimming and sweating like a madman, but I wasn't listening to my GUT. It was trying to tell me all along that I was out of control, obsessed to the point of panic. By focusing so much on one area of my life, I was injuring the other areas. It was "uncontrolled failure." I was losing touch with my overall life purpose.

I reviewed that book religiously, and everything I wrote down in that book happened. I finished my last two years strong, starting at offensive guard, and received academic All-Conference honors two years in a row. I was nominated for the Brian Piccolo award my senior year and lost to a kid who had brain cancer from Clemson University. I received numerous honors and awards academically and graduated from Georgia Tech with honors. In the end I had a chance to play in the NFL as a free agent, but my GUT told me to take a different direction.

It all worked out and changed my life for the good. I will forever be grateful for the simple process that Coach Curry taught me. I'm thankful that I learned how to listen to my GUT about patience and controlled, purposeful hard work. Coach Curry helped me get in tune with my GUT, change my trajectory, and come back from what I thought was hopeless failure.

I recommend that you try Coach Curry's process for achieving your own "crazy big goals." I know it worked for me. But please remember the key to it all is to listen to your GUT. My GUT guided me all through the process. If I followed the steps deliberately, my GUT felt great. If I didn't, my GUT would tell me—I would feel that deep-down twinge of self-disgust, that emotional downer that I wasn't doing what was right for myself.

The goals I set felt right. The behaviors I chose felt right. I set myself up for "controlled failure," because I knew I would be pushing my limits, but my GUT wouldn't have it any other way. Furthermore, my GUT told me if I was out of balance or going too far in one direction or the other. I think one reason I blew out my shoulders in the first place was that I was into "uncontrolled failure." Of course my GUT told me I shouldn't wreck my body, but I did it anyway, and I paid a very heavy price for it.

The GUT is that deep down voice of balance. It says "Work hard, but stay in control. Be smart. Don't underdo, but don't overdo either. Remember that you're more than just a body or a mind or a heart or a soul—you're all of those things."

There is great wisdom in the GUT. Listen to it, and you'll be winning every step of the way.

Go With Your GUT!

Answer these questions for yourself. Write down your answers.

1. Are there changes you really ought to make in your life, but you've hesitated because you're afraid of failure?

2. "I have failed over and over and over again in my life. And that is why I succeed." Can you explain why Michael Jordan, the world's greatest basketball player, would say such a thing?

3. When in your life has failure actually turned out to be a good thing? What have you learned from failure?

4. Have you ever done something like Coach Curry recommends? What are your "crazy big goals" for your Mind, Heart, Body, and Soul? What is your GUT telling you?

PART 4

LEAD WITH GUTS!

GUTsy Leadership, GUTsy Goals, and GUTsy Teams

CHAPTER 11

Leading the Way

What does it mean to "lead with GUTs?" Most real leaders don't have titles—they're the people you look up to every day who have GUTs. Maybe it's your boss, but it's just as likely to be the person in the office next to yours, or your old schoolteacher, or a grandparent.

So far we've talked about leading your *own* GUTsy life.

Now let's talk about being a GUTsy leader of other people.

Everybody's a leader. You're a leader. It doesn't matter if you're the CEO of a large corporation, or a team leader at work, or a parent at home with your children – you're a leader. Somebody looks to you to lead the way, whether it's a whole company, a small team, or a couple of kids. Even if you don't have a leadership title, you're still a leader, because at some time or another people will rely on you to take the lead.

If you don't think you're a leader, think again. Was Rosa Parks a leader? She didn't have a title. She was a lowly textile worker. Does that mean she was less of a leader? Was Gandhi a leader? He never in his life held any kind of title or office. But didn't he lead a major change in the world? What made these people leaders, despite the odds against them?

They had GUTs.

You have a choice: You can lead with GUTs or without. The difference between the two? Only leaders with GUTs are truly effective leaders.

What does it mean to "lead with GUTs"? I think it means three things:

A GUTsy leader has a good character. One of the key points of this book is that deep down inside you is a voice that tells you what's right. If you learn to listen to it, your GUT tells you what you should do when the choice is between showing love or ill will. Or between compromising your principles or standing up for them. Or between taking responsibility or ducking it.

A GUTsy leader has big GUTsy goals. You become a change agent, "the tipping point," the person who "turns the ship around." You shake things up because you have a certain place to go—it comes from your GUT. It's the crazy, big GUTsy goal that possesses *you*, obsesses *you*, and loves *you*. You focus on that goal with all of your might. You get down into the details. You find out what it takes to get there, and you never take your eyes off that destination.

A GUTsy leader grows the team. Your team is a true "huddle." Everybody counts, every contribution matters. You deliberately capitalize on the unique powers, talents, and capabilities of each team member. You make tough decisions, but you leave most decisions to the team. How they will ever grow if they don't become leaders themselves?

Let's find out whether you have the GUTs to be a GUTsy leader. Take this little quiz:

LEADERSHIP AND GUTS

True or false

1. Great leaders focus only on the big picture.

2. GUTsy leaders push to achieve many goals.

3. A leader with GUTs pays no attention to the naysayers.

4. Great leaders show love.

5. GUTsy leaders are humble.

6. GUTsy leaders let their team members make most decisions.

7. Great leaders show a lot of grit.

8. Great leaders spend a lot of time celebrating successes.

9. Leaders with GUTs are no-nonsense, kick-butt-and-take-names people.

10. Great leaders have the GUTs to take responsibility for results.

I am   1) Not likely   2) Pretty unlikely   3) Could go one way or the other   4) Pretty likely   5) Very likely to do the following:

11. Avoid conflict and confrontation.

12. Rescue people who are having problems.

13. Do my best to please everyone.

14. Include as many different viewpoints as possible when making decisions.

15. Treat all people as my equals.

16. Listen to all sides in a conflict.

17. Look for ways to shake up the status quo.

18. Avoid doing jobs other people can do.

19. Withdraw from making tough decisions.

20. Show love to everyone.

Take 5 points for each correct true or false answer for questions 1-10. Key: 1F 2F 3F 4T 5T 6T 7F 8T 9F 10T

Reverse score on 11, 12, 13, 19.

Enter your score here: _____

If your score is...	Then you are...
91-100	A GUTsy leader! You have a trustworthy character, a clear, strong sense of purpose, and an instinct for maximizing the potential of your team. You care deeply about each person on the team. You're willing to take the right kind of risks to grow other people and achieve your big GUTsy goals.
81-90	An average leader. You go along with whatever there is to go along with, whether it's the right thing to do or not. You avoid shaking things up. You have quotas or goals but you don't really "own" them—you're not personally excited about them. Your team does what it does, whatever that is. It's all kind of . . . empty.
71-80	Not really up to it yet. You're probably scared and will do anything to stay out of trouble. You do what it takes to survive, but aren't sure what that is from day to day. You either avoid your team or hover over them to make sure they don't make trouble for you.
0-70	No GUTs. You have an unstable character. Your goals shift around a lot—if you even have any goals. You're not really interested in growing your team's capabilities so they can be leaders too. You need to get help if you want to be a successful leader!

Now let's drill down on those three essentials of a GUTsy leader.

A GUTsy Leader Has Character

People think of a "GUTsy" leader as a no-nonsense person who shoots first and asks no questions later. He or she yells a lot, kicks butt, and takes names.

But leaders like this aren't GUTsy; in fact, they have no GUTs. They're usually insecure themselves—fearful of failure, they adopt an aggressive, domineering style to show they're "in charge."

GUTless parents shout at their kids and hit them to make sure they know who's "boss." GUTless managers lord it over their employees and blame them when things go wrong. GUTless CEOs "take full responsibility" for failures but get their bonuses anyway. So kids grow up angry, work teams become resentful, and employees turn cynical. Natural consequences.

You wouldn't expect it, but a truly GUTsy leader is humble and full of love. I know that doesn't sound right.

Here's an example. A little French auto-parts manufacturing firm was dying, and the parent company sent out a young engineer named Jean-François to figure out how to revive it or else how to close it down. He had never led anything before, much less a whole company.

So instead of pretending he was this big genius turnaround artist, he met with the employees, told them he had no idea what to do, and asked their advice.

They were shocked. Nobody had ever asked *them* before what they thought. It turned out they had a *lot* of thoughts. Surprising everyone, within a year the company—FAVI S.A.—had made a sharp turnaround. Their clients were delighted. The employees were full of energy. Over the years, the company won awards for the quality of their work. Against all odds, FAVI became a prosperous international company.

What did Jean-François do to make such a difference?

Because he's a humble person, he listened really hard to the people who actually did the work. He listened to the clients. He didn't try to force his own ideas on anybody (after all, he didn't have any). He was humble enough to learn.

Because he's a loving person, he trusted his people. He found out that all the tools in the factory were locked up. The previous manager was afraid the employees would steal them, so they had to request a tool if they needed it. The first thing Jean-François did was to unlock the tool cabinet.

He also found out they hated the time clock. They were docked pay even if they were a few minutes late or needed to leave a few minutes early. So Jean-François ripped out the time clock.

These were risky, GUTsy things to do. The employees could have taken advantage of their boss, but that didn't happen. When they were no longer treated like cheaters, they stepped up and did better work than they'd ever done.

Even GUTsier stuff followed: He found other jobs for the company accountants, middle managers, and even the sales force. He trusted the people who did the actual manufacturing to do their own accounts, manage themselves, and communicate with the clients. Jean-François says, "Conventional management believes that people are bad. If you lock everything up, you create thieves. If you have a time clock, you assume a worker will be deliberately late. That means you assume he's a cheat. But he's not a cheat. It's profoundly unfair. We simply assume that people are good, and we trust them to do the right thing."

If you ask Jean-François why FAVI is in business, he says, "To do meaningful work and to give and receive love. Yes, *love*, a word rarely heard in the world of business."

At FAVI, they give a little extra love to their customers. For example, at Christmastime they mold excess brass into little Christmas figurines and put them in with the product, imagining that someone somewhere will find them. Is it any wonder that FAVI's customers love them? [59]

It takes a lot of GUTs to show love.

It takes a lot of GUTs to show love because it's risky. You expose yourself to loss and pain and betrayal. You commit yourself to other people who might not commit to you.

Jean-François is a GUTsy leader. Listening made him a leader. Love made him a leader.

"In the past five years, loving as a leadership skill has been suggested by educators and CEOs," says Greg Stebbins, a nationally known business writer. "We are talking about the form of loving referred to by the Greeks as *agape* love, not the romantic kind of loving. This type of loving has more to do with how a person behaves towards another, not our feelings about them. It implies a selfless relationship, not an ego-based relationship." [60]

A GUTsy leader builds character into the team. He or she teaches the team how to take risks and show

---

59 Laloux, Reinventing Organizations, Nelson Parker, 2014, 202.

60 Stebbins, Gregory, "Letting Wisdom Lead: Are You Leading With Your Heart and Your GUT?" Huffington Post, May 14, 2013. http://www. huffingtonpost.com/gregory-stebbins/letting-wisdom-lead-are-y_b_2878813.html

Lead With Humility

In my early days I didn't understand the role of compassion in helping people overcome their fears. Twenty years ago I might have looked down on someone who was experiencing a rough time and then ask myself and others why the person let him or herself get that way. Now I wonder about what might have contributed to the person getting to a low point.

It was probably self-pride that limited me from showing empathy toward people during my early leadership days. I remember being extremely prideful and buying a house because it had a three hundred foot driveway and I wanted everybody to be impressed as they walked up the driveway.

Self-pride is arguably one of the first things leaders might need to deal with. I'm not suggesting that we shouldn't be proud of our accomplishments, but pride that's self-serving is really a form of arrogance that can easily get in the way of a leader's potential for success. Leaders might need to self-reflect to determine whether self-pride is hindering their leadership progress.

-Peter Grandich, CEO, Grandich & Co., Wall Street brokers

From "The DNA of Gutsy Leaders," August 18, 2015. http:// www.petergrandich.com/the-dna-of-gutsy-leaders-a-must-read/

love. One company has a huddle every day where they ask one question: "What can we do today to show our customers we love them?" They come up with all kinds of surprises, from handing out flowers to carrying purchases out to the car—just little things that show love.

Another company has a "day of thanking." Employees get a day off and an envelope with $200 in cash to spend any way they want to show gratitude to somebody important to them. When they come back, they go around the room and tell their stories of what happened.[61]

When you show love, you become vulnerable. You lay yourself open to very deep hurt. That's why it's the GUTsiest thing of all. Like Jean-François says, people don't put "love" and "business" in the same sentence. But he does. The more you show love to the people with whom you work and do business, the more you will love them. That takes GUTs.

A leader with GUTs also stands up for his team.

You'll remember that Kyle Bjornstad's Oregon State basketball team had a terrible season his junior year. It didn't help that the coach didn't stand up for the team. He told them they were terrible players, called them names, threatened to kick everybody off the team. No wonder the team was demoralized. Kyle took all he could stand and finally got in the coach's face: "We're a family! Stop treating your family like this! These guys are giving all they've got!" Kyle figured that was the end of his own basketball career, but a few days later the coach was fired.

The coach's replacement, Craig Robinson, was exactly what was needed. He never demeaned his players. He treated the players like a father, preached accountability, and instilled a discipline that was lacking. "You will be in class every day. In fact, you will sit in the front row. You will be at practice at 5 a.m. every day. We are a family. We're together." And he turned that team around.

---

61 Laloux, 218

A leader with GUTs also stands up for what's right.

Jack Kemp, who was quarterback of the San Diego Chargers and later on a U.S. Senator, learned about GUTsy leadership from his legendary coach Sid Gillman. This was back in the 1960s when blacks were treated shamefully unequally in parts of the country.

"The most important part of leading with GUTs is character. Character involves knowing what you stand for and what you are willing to stand *up* for."

–David Dotlich, strategist and consultant

One time the Chargers were playing in Houston and Coach Gillman took the whole team to a movie. Kemp says he sat down and noticed that four of his teammates were missing. It turned out they had been sent up to the "blacks-only" balcony. "When I told Coach Gillman, he stood immediately and said, 'OK, you guys, we're out of here.' In a silent, powerful demonstration of our belief in equality, living and working as a team, we walked out as a team. I was very proud of Coach Gillman." [62]

Sid Gillman literally stood up for what's right, and that's what GUTsy leaders do. If you're going to be a GUTsy leader, you know deep down in your GUT what's right and wrong and what you're willing to stand up for.

One of the big problems in our country is GUTless leaders— CEOs who take giant salaries while their companies cheat their customers, officials who make promises they won't keep, politicians who cheat on their spouses and then criticize other politicians for doing the same thing, bosses who don't care

---

62 Kemp, Jack, "The Inspiration of the Football Huddle," Chicken Soup for the Soul, n.d. http://www.chickensoup.com/book-story/48240/the-inspiration-of-the-football-huddle

about their people. Nearly half of American workers have left a job because of the boss—does that surprise anybody? [63]

Love, humility, keeping commitments, standing for what's right—these are the qualities of a leader with character. These are the qualities of a GUTsy leader.

Go With Your GUT!

Answer these questions for yourself. Write down your answers.

1. What experiences do you have with GUTsy leaders? Did they "lead from the GUT" as described in this chapter? What about GUTless leaders?

2. "People don't put 'love' and 'business' in the same sentence." Do you think that's true? Do you have any experience with a "loving business"?

3. Does it surprise you that the character of a GUTsy leader is to be humble and full of love? What makes that kind of leader "GUTsy"? Does it describe your approach to leadership?

4. In what ways are you a leader? Are you a GUTsy leader?

---

63 Risen, Tom, "Why Workers Hate Their Bosses," U.S. News & World Report, April 3, 2015. http://www.usnews.com/news/blogs/data-mine/2015/04/03/why-workers-hate-their-bosses

CHAPTER 12

GUTsy Leaders Have Big GUTsy Goals

People go crazy without hope, without something meaningful to work toward. Everyone needs a big GUTsy goal that makes a big difference in their world. It doesn't matter if you're a genius CEO or a mom and dad who love their kids—you can't lead people without GUTsy goals. Otherwise, they choke on the aimlessness of life. How many of us, deep down in our GUT, know that we're not really making a difference . . . yet?

Leaders with GUTs have crystal-clear, big GUTsy goals that make a difference in the world. There's usually only one—sometimes two or three, but there shouldn't be more than that. There's the old saying, "If you chase two rabbits, you won't catch either one."

We've talked about what it means to live from the GUT. We've seen individuals—like Kyle Bjornstad, Jeni Bauer, Beethoven and Andy from *Shawshank Redemption*—who have that Big What, that primary goal that wells up from inside.

Now let's see how to achieve GUTsy goals together.

How do you tell a GUTsy team or organization apart from a so-so team? Most people belong to so-so teams, if you believe the data that says about half of us hate our jobs.[64] Why? Because they're meaningless. There's nothing to work for except a salary. What difference does it make?

One person put it this way: "You feel like what you're doing doesn't matter to you, your coworkers, or to your company. Instead, your efforts feel like busy work just to fill time. You don't have real motivation to do much, and find yourself quickly losing interest in your job. It is difficult to throw an immense amount of time into a pursuit you don't care about." [65]

Even the people at the top of the corporate world are drifting around feeling useless. "Behind the façade and the bravado, the lives of powerful corporate leaders are ones of quiet suffering too. Their frantic activity is often a poor cover up for a deep inner sense of emptiness. . . . At both the top and bottom, organizations are more often than not playfields for unfulfilling pursuits . . . inhospitable to the deeper yearnings of our souls." [66]

So many of us are running around being busy but making no difference. Why?

Here's my theory. It's due to GUTless leadership. Most leaders— from the top execs to the store manager—are too scared to commit to making a difference. They're afraid somebody will hold them to it.

That's why most companies have stupid mission statements. They're showy, empty promises that don't require anybody to do anything.

- "We are committed to being the world's best (fill in the blank) company." (How will we ever know if we're the best? Maybe we're the worst. Does anybody know how to measure "best"?)

---

64 Brownstone, "Everyone in the World Hates Their Jobs."

65 Jhang, Maggie, Here's Why So Many People Hate Their Jobs," Business Insider, June 19, 2014. http://www.businessinsider.com/reasons-you-hate-your-job-2014-6

66 Laloux, 4.

- "Our goal is to enhance the quality of life of our customers and employees." (OK, people, get out there and do some enhancing, whatever that means.)

- "Our mission is to empower our people to give value to our customers with integrity." (Well, at least that's better than micromanaging your employees and ripping off your customers.)

These goals are GUTless. They inspire nobody. What they really mean is, "Our goal is to get enough dorks to buy our stuff so we can make a living." At least that would be honest.

My friend is a business consultant who meets periodically with top executives of major corporations. He told me about one well-known CEO who sat behind his giant mahogany table in his expensive suit, pontificating on his "grand vision" for turning around the company and his "big picture" and his "world-class strategy"—and a few months later was fired for getting nothing done.

GUTsy leaders don't play these silly games. They look inside themselves for what really matters— to themselves and to the team. They

Big GUTsy Goals

What does a big GUTsy goal look like?

"We will create a 'smart phone' that will be much more than a phone—it will perform any task you need it to do!" –Apple team who created the iPhone

"My kids will grow up to love serving others above all. That will happen as we travel the world actually doing hands-on service for people who are not as fortunate as we are." –A wealthy dad who didn't want his kids spoiled by wealth

"I will show Jim Crow for the criminal he is and what he has done to one life multiplied millions of times over these United States and the world." –Rosa Parks

"This nation should commit itself to achieving the goal, before this decade is out, of landing a man on the moon and returning him safely to the earth." –John F. Kennedy

"Help me, Obi Wan-Kenobi. You're my only hope. You must see this droid safely delivered to Alderaan."

–Princess Leia

make a hard commitment to a diamond-hard goal that makes a big difference in their world.

"Only when love and need are one is the deed ever really done."

–Robert Frost

The big GUTsy goal comes from the GUT, of course. The people at Apple who created the first smartphone had a thrilling dream: to create something you could hold in your hand that would do everything you could ever want it to do! Talk to people, take photos, play music and movies, find your way in the dark, tell you where you are and where you're going—and a million other tasks. I *love* my smartphone. The only thing it can't do is make me a sandwich. Who knows . . . maybe someday?

Now, the smartphone was a big GUTsy goal. It was a big cause you could believe in. The folks at Apple struggled under unbelievable pressure to deliver the iPhone on time. It was "total war." For two-and-a-half years at Apple, nothing else mattered. Andy Grignon, one of the top engineers, remembers, "It was just a mess, but it was great!" [67]

GUTsy goals require total concentration. GUTsy goals shake everything up. GUTsy goals are all about the big cause everybody believes in deep down inside. "GUTsy leaders in today's business world embody the same spirit as Rosa Parks. They *provoke change* by going against outdated norms that prevent them from playing a bigger game and realizing their cause." [68] The GUTsy goal of Rosa Parks was to show the world how bad segregation was and not to take it anymore. She provoked change—that's the heart of a big GUTsy goal.

---

67 Vogelstein, Fred, "And Then Steve Said, 'Let There Be an iPhone,' New York Times Magazine, October 4, 2013.

68 Corcoran, Denise, "Leading from GUTs Builds GUTsy Organizations," The Empowered Blog, n.d. http://www.empoweredbusiness.com/leading-from-GUTs-builds-GUTsy-organizations/

I'm acquainted with a man who has a lot of money—I mean, *a lot of money.* He also has seven children. They know their dad could buy them an island in the Caribbean and staff it with servants and bring them anything their hearts desire. But Dad had a GUTsy goal for his family that had nothing to do with luxury islands.

He wanted his kids to grow up to serve others and to love it. From the time they were little, he would take them on trips around the world, but not to play—to work! In a poor Asian village, the kids worked in an eye clinic helping take care of patients. In a Peruvian town, they helped build houses for single mothers. In Africa, they dug wells and distributed donated mosquito nets. The kids are now almost grown up. They are very rich kids, but you wouldn't know it. They're totally into community service. That's how they spend their days, and it would be hard to find young people who are happier or more at peace.

People need a cause. Without big GUTsy goals they go crazy. They invent things to do. They pretend that what they're doing is really important when it isn't. If they're nice, they drop their dumb stuff to help you with your dumb stuff. They'll do anything to please you, and they get awards at the company party for being so pleasant and helpful. It's the next best thing to actually doing something worthwhile.

GUTsy leaders don't settle for anything less than the big game, the cause they love, the Big Why and the Big What. "It's the place where your deep gladness meets the world's deep hunger," as the writer Frederick Buechner said. The world is hungry for the best you have to give—don't ever think otherwise.

Big GUTsy goals are so clear you'd have to be a doorknob to misunderstand them. Frodo has to throw the ring into Mount Doom. Luke Skywalker's team has to destroy the Death Star. Marlin has to find Nemo. Everything they do is driven by that one aim. They might not start out as odds-on leaders, but the One Goal makes them leaders.

Go With Your GUT!

Answer these questions for yourself. Write down your answers.

1. Does your company or your team or work group have a mission statement? Is it dumb or meaningful? Does it inspire you? Does it move you, down in your GUT? If not, what kind of a statement would?

2. Have you ever felt deep down in your GUT that you were wasting time even when you were busy? That what you were doing didn't really make a difference? What did it feel like?

3. Does your work team or your family have a crystal-clear, big GUTsy goal? If not, what does your GUT tell you it should be? What do they think it should be? Should there be more than one goal?

CHAPTER 13

A GUTsy Leader Grows People

A GUTsy leader is not what you'd expect—a big blustering presence that takes giant risks. GUTsy leaders are humble people full of love, who care so much about their team members and their potential that they want to see them grow into GUTsy leaders themselves. But GUTsy leaders don't abandon people to sink or swim—they huddle with them constantly to inspire them and motivate commitment. They actively look for people with the unique powers needed to achieve big GUTsy goals.

If you love people, you want them to grow. Otherwise, they die.

Please don't get me wrong. Loving people is not the same as "pleasing" them. To love a person doesn't mean that you do everything they want or do everything for them. It doesn't mean that you avoid disagreeing with them when you have to. And it doesn't mean rescuing them from a challenge instead of letting them figure it out on their own.

If you love people, you *let* them grow.

Once when I was standing in line at the airport, I started a conversation with the man in front of me. He was an agronomist—a high-tech farmer—from the Netherlands who

175

specialized in hydroponic gardens, or growing vegetables in water. I asked him how they tasted. He said, "They're good, but not as good as vegetables grown in the earth." I asked him why. He said, "Because of the pressure of the soil, plants have to fight for water and nutrients." This constant struggle, he told me, is what gives a ripe, fresh vegetable its wonderful flavor.

The same is true for people. It's the struggle that gives flavor to life and that ripens and matures our abilities. So a GUTsy leader doesn't go around rescuing the team members from hardships—not if she wants a GUTsy team.

A GUTsy leader hands responsibility over to the team. At FAVI, Jean-François won't make decisions for the workers. He says, "I am not responsible for what you do. You are responsible—to the client and to each other. So you need to lead out. You need to make the decisions. You are the leaders here." (That takes a lot of GUTs!) Once the boss stopped deciding everything, performance soared. All of the energy and time wasted trying to please the boss went into pleasing customers.

Jean-François sees himself as just another resource for the work teams at FAVI. There are certain things only he as CEO can do, like signing contracts, so the teams tell him what they need and he delivers—not the other way around. They do all the goal-setting, hiring and firing, organizing, ordering parts and tools, accounting, and communicating with clients.

I hope you can see how unusually GUTsy Jean-François is. Some would say he's taking huge risks by letting his people run the company; but because he believes people are basically good, he's willing to take that risk.

"GUTsy leaders are game changers; they redefine the game, defy mediocrity, declare war on complacency, explore the uncharted, risk the unthinkable, and do the unconventional."

–Jackie and Kevin Freiberg, leadership consultants.

And if you were to watch the workers in their huddles, you'd see real growth in their power to achieve and their pride in their achievements. When there's an issue to resolve, the team leader calls out, and they huddle. When it's time to celebrate a success, they call a huddle and party.

But the key huddles are held almost daily. In these huddles they do exactly what we do in football. They look at the score to see if they're winning. They put their heads together on what to do next to make sure they do win. And they commit to each other on exactly what each worker will do to make it happen.

The next day they huddle all over again.

The power of the huddle is amazing.

Years ago, I learned firsthand the meaning of the huddle while I was playing football at Georgia Tech.

In football each player has unique powers and a different job to do, and it takes the collective effort of eleven guys doing their job to make each play work every time. The huddle is where that collective effort comes together.

In the Southern states football is a very big deal, and at Georgia Tech we played some of the toughest schools in college football: Notre Dame, Alabama, Clemson, Florida, Auburn, and Georgia, among others. These teams always had great athletes four deep. It seemed like every week we were playing a nationally ranked team.

Playing at Tech was great and painful at the same time—great because I loved football, and playing in big games in front of thousands of people was thrilling—but painful because we lost a lot, at least at first.

The odds ran heavily against us.

In the five years I was at Tech we went from one of the worst teams in college football to one of the best. The amazing thing

The Huddle

The football huddle is a metaphor for our culture, imperfect like all metaphors...

The men who earn a place in the huddle have learned the miracle of team. The training camp experience is unbelievable, two a day, three a day practices in the heat ... everybody thinks about quitting. Trust me—everybody.

We learn ever so slowly that our differences do not matter in the huddle. When we trudge in after each interminable workout, we know that sweat smells the same on everybody's body. When we get busted in the mouth, that blood that trickles is the same color. Everybody's tired. Everybody's hurt.

It is in this process that the miracle occurs. Men who have been raised to hate each other's guts become brothers. I've seen racists reformed. I've seen the most unlikely hugs after victories or losses. I've seen inner-city kids invite country boys from the mountains to come home with them for Thanksgiving dinner, and I've seen those invitations accepted—and reciprocated, thus changing parents' lives.

Our players become brothers for life. It's what America could be, might be, should be in our best dreams.

-Coach Bill Curry
https://www.youtube.com/watch?v=IGuFy2TBlag

178

is we did it with a huddle full of average, hard-working kids who played from their GUTs.

Our success was born in the huddle. We eleven players beat each other to near death every day in practice. We almost ripped out our pecs competing with each other in the weight room. We insulted each other's moms and damned each other to hell and learned to love each other far better than most brothers do.

And once you're in the huddle with your brothers, nothing matters but the Big What: the score on the big board. You depend on all the different powers in the huddle – the quarterback with the infallible GUT instinct, the wide receiver who is as graceful as a ballet dancer, the offensive lineman as heavy as a horse, and even the "friendly giant" center who connects every time. You could not care less who's black or white, Christian or Muslim, gay or straight or liberal or conservative. Each man is uniquely powerful. Each contribution is priceless.

In the South during football season, every Saturday is hot and humid. Playing four quarters of a football game with a field temperature of 120 degrees takes a toll on your body—and that's just the start. You're running around smashing into giants who want to kill you and your family. The collisions are brutal. Things break and bleed and get quite nasty.

Then it happens. Late in the game you're behind by a few points and there is only a little time left on the clock. You get the ball deep in your own territory, and you and the ten other guys in the huddle have one last chance.

You take the field exhausted, your legs cramping, broken fingers sticking out in odd directions, and blood everywhere. You got nothing in the tank. You're empty, and you have no idea how you're going to block that giant who's been kicking your ass all day and saying terrible things about your mother.

Then something magical happens to you. You look around the huddle at your best friends you've played with for years. You have suffered much alongside each other, you have spent countless hours in the weight room together, going to 5 a.m. workouts, pushing each other past all reasonable limits on and off the field.

Time slows down as you look around into the eyes of your teammates, and you see that they are just as empty and broken as you are. One of them probably doesn't even know where he is because earlier in the game he took a head shot that would kill most people. You connect with him eye to eye, soul to soul, and know—*deep down inside, you just know*—that he will find a way to do his job or die trying. He won't let you down.

Then you realize that if *he* can do it, *you* can do it. It's the ultimate GUT check. After a few more glances and a few more GUT checks, everyone in the huddle is on the same page. Peace and calm comes over the entire group, then we get these shit-eating grins on our faces because we know that with all our hearts, souls, and GUTs, we're going for victory.

Then you march down that damn field, and with just a few seconds on the clock you punch it in the end zone for the win. The home crowd erupts, the clock goes to zero, and victory is yours. You lie exhausted on the field, the fans storm the field and tear down the goal post—it is surreal and almost unbelievable.

Afterward, as you watch the game films, you realize that you played far above your capacity. You realize how much you have grown personally and how much the team has grown. Together, with love in your heart for each other, you pulled it out of your GUTs! That's the power of the huddle.

The great thing about the huddle is the love. I was a white homeless guy from Las Vegas. There were a couple of Southern white achievers who came from the manicured suburbs. There were black dudes off the streets of the inner cities. We couldn't have been more different. These are guys who wouldn't have even talked to each other before the huddle. Now we love each other. We grew up together. Years later we still talk to each other, share our thoughts and problems and worries and hopes, laugh and cry together, because we are still a *huddle*.

In the tribalized society we live in where people are withdrawing more and more into their own corners, we talk a lot about what divides us. We talk a good deal about race and inequality, about how our racial and religious and ethnic and political differences shouldn't matter, but the conflicts just get more intense.

What we need in this country is the power of the huddle.

In the huddle, those social differences just don't matter. The late, great San Diego quarterback Jack Kemp knew all about it. "Any difference in race, creed and class immediately dissolves in the common aim of a team win. Divisiveness only weakens a team. It has no place in a huddle, on or off the field.

"A successful team walks onto the field with issues of race, religion, and all societal pressures ratcheted down to inconsequential by the strength of common goals." [69]

Of course, some differences do matter in the huddle— differences in power and ability. As on a winning football team,

---

69 Kemp, Jack,"The Inspiration of the Football Huddle."

everybody has unique powers and all of those powers are needed. The quarterback needs the linemen. The receiver needs the quarterback. Everyone depends on each other's distinctive abilities. What makes those differences important is the *goal*.

It takes GUTs to break out of your corner and join the huddle, because a lot of the people in the huddle may be very different from you. They might be of a different race. Maybe you're uncomfortable working with people of a different sexual orientation. Maybe you dislike their politics or their religion upsets you.

But none of that matters in the huddle. When you have a Big What —a big GUTsy goal to chase—you need their diverse powers and strengths and capacities.

Here's a little quiz you can take to find out if you have the GUTs to include people instead of pushing them away.

DIVERSITY AND GUTS

True or false

1. There is no difference in intelligence among races.

2. People who get harassed for wearing religious clothing are asking for it.

3. Women are not as serious about their careers as men are.

4. Religious freedom should apply to all religions.

5. All people are "created equal."

6. Most stereotypes are true.

7. Minorities get unfair advantages.

8. If you say you don't "see" race, you are ignoring racism.

9. People who complain about racism are just being over-sensitive.

10. As a rule, Muslims are dangerous people.

BEHAVIORAL

I am 1) Not likely 2) Pretty unlikely 3) Could go one way or the other 4) Pretty likely 5) Very likely to do the following:

11. Tell jokes about race.

12. Befriend a person who is a member of a minority group.

13. Tell sexual jokes about certain people.

14. Speak up for someone being harassed because of race, gender, age, or sexual orientation.

15. Make fun of members of minority groups if they're not around.

16. Let someone who is being threatened with harassment know that I am available to help.

17. Actively seek to get to know people who are different from me in terms of race, ethnic background, gender, religion, or sexual orientation.

18. Speak up if I see a person of a different religion being harassed.

19. Laugh at racist or sexist jokes.

20. Avoid people who are different from me.

Take 5 points for each correct true or false answer for questions 1-10. Key: 1T 2F 3F 4T 5T 6F 7F 8T 9F 10F

Reverse score on 11, 13, 15, 19, 20

Enter your score here: _____

If your score is...	Then...
91-100	It takes GUTs to stand up for everybody and benefit from their unique gifts and powers, and you have GUTs!
81-90	You're not as brave as you ought to be about including people who are different from you and standing up for them when they're not around.
71-80	You probably like to pretend that racism and sexism are things of the past and not worth worrying about. You miss the rewards of having a lot of diverse people around you and benefiting from their diverse strengths.
0-70	No GUTs. You exclude people, laugh at them, or bully them—or allow other people to do so—either because you're afraid of people who are different from you, or because deep down inside you think you're better than they are. In either case, you need help.

Jack Kemp used to talk about how his experiences in the huddle helped him understand African-Americans. "The huddle is colorblind," he would say. He was a lot less worried about the linemen's race than about their power to keep him from getting killed by the opposing linemen.

The secret to the power of the huddle is in the power of the common goal. One college student says she attended a very diverse college, but the students "hung out in groups where everyone was the same." She was also an AmeriCorps volunteer and discovered that where teams worked together, "members truly served and socialized across racial, ethnic, and class lines." [70]

So how can we improve race relations in this country? Stop thinking about race and start thinking about what we can do together. Pick a goal everyone can love—people of different backgrounds. Could blacks and whites together create a team to fight illegal drugs? How about getting Hispanic and non-

---

[70] Waldman, Steven, "Sweating to the Oldies," US News & World Report, May 24, 2011.

Who's in Your Huddle?

Your personal huddle should be people who inspire, motivate, and challenge you. They have the knowledge to counsel and advise you. They have strengths you don't have.

When choosing your huddle, ask:

"The underlying proposition of a personal board of directors is to gain insight and wisdom from people you have always looked up to or aspired to be."

"How much do you think you can learn from someone who is exactly like you? Probably not a lot. Include those people who have inspired you despite their starkly different personalities and ways of thinking. The more people there are with different approaches, the more room there is to learn."

"Include at least one member who knows you well—a person who is aware of your temperament, thinking style and ambitions in life would be in a better position to advise you and give you honest feedback."

From Bailey, Simon T., "How to Create Your Personal Board of Directors," Fast Company, December 5, 2014.

Hispanic high school kids together to repair rundown houses for low-income people? Stop talking, get in a huddle, and do something worthwhile as a team—that will do more to solve the diversity problem than anything else.

I started this book by telling you about my terrible childhood, and about the counselor who told me I should be in prison, insane, or dead. She asked me how I'd managed to make my life a success even though I started my life like one of the "Sons of Anarchy" – a really bad one.

You'll recall that I told her there were two reasons I didn't end up dead under a wrecked motorcycle and full of bullets.

The first was my ability to listen to what my GUT was telling me.

The second was my "personal huddle"—the handful of powerful, positive people I rely on to help me achieve my goals. That huddle now includes more than just my old teammates – it also includes my family and some of my co-workers and friends at church. They are coaches, teachers, doctors, lawyers, writers, mechanics, financial experts; generous people I can huddle with to advise me and help me grow mentally, emotionally, and spiritually.

Everyone in my huddle brings something powerful to me that I don't have—gifts, talents, experience, and insights that I need to thrive. Without my huddle, I'd be floating in a ditch somewhere.

The huddle saved my life.

Everybody who wants to succeed in life needs a personal huddle. You need a huddle.

Go With Your GUT!

Answer these questions for yourself. Write down your answers.

1. When have you been part of a team that "played from the GUT"? Have you ever been part of a "huddle"? What was it like? In what ways did you grow personally?

2. What would you do if you were the leader of a huddle at work? What would be your agenda? What would you want the outcome to be?

3. What do you think about your score on the Diversity and Guts quiz? Do you have attitudes you need to work on? What do you think would be the scores of the people you work with?

4. Who should you invite to be in your personal huddle? Where are you weak? What do you need help with? Which people in your life have the power to help you achieve your goals? What is your GUT telling you?

CONCLUSION

The GUTsy Life

From business executives trying to hit the must-reach numbers to people trying to lose weight, everybody knows it's easy to set a goal, but achieving it is an entirely different story. It takes GUTS— tenacity, excitement, and strong "GUTsy" decisions. In this book you learned how to actually get there—how to fulfill your life's purpose with energy, love, and determination.

This book has been all about living a "GUTsy" life.

People say to me, "I like what you say about listening to my GUT and following it, but I'm not very GUTsy. I'm too timid, too young, too old, too fat and out of shape or too thin and out of shape. I don't have the confidence to be GUTsy. I'm afraid to be GUTsy."

As you finish reading this book, I want to be very clear about what it means to be "GUTsy."

Business people talk about "GUTsy" calls. In sports we talk about "GUTsy" plays. In politics they talk about "GUTsy" decisions.

I feel that there are two ways of being "GUTsy," one of them good, one of them not so good.

Here's an example of a good GUTsy call. One week the Atlanta Falcons found themselves in a critical overtime against the New Orleans Saints. On a fourth-and-one from his own 29-yard line, Coach Mike Smith "rolled the dice" and sent the ball in the hands of a powerful running back right up the middle toward the end zone.

It didn't work, and the Falcons lost the game.

Why do I say it was a good GUTsy call?

Because Mike Smith took a reasonable shot, made an odd, quirky move, and even though he lost out, he tried for something truly exceptional.

Furthermore, as sports writer Adam Lazarus says, "Those types of on-field, in-game decisions—not draft choices, trades, firings, cuts, free-agent signings, etc.—are the very definition of GUTsy. They are made, quite literally, on their 'GUT,' not with the aid of weeks of thought or a collection of big brains in a room looking at a draft board." [71]

The Falcons under GUTsy Mike Smith went on to win more than 80 percent of their games the next season.

By contrast, there are bad ways of being "GUTsy."

- Tony Allen, a grandstanding NBA player, famously decided to run for a slam dunk after the official stopped the game, but then blew out his knee and missed the dunk anyway.

- Or Pete Rose, the baseball great who placed illegal bets on his own team and lost his place in the Baseball Hall of Fame.

- Or Rosie Ruiz, who came in first in the Boston Marathon of 1980, until it was revealed that she had started the

---

71 Lazarus, Adam, "The 10 GUTsiest Calls in NFL History," BR Bleacher Report, November 17, 2011. http://bleacherreport.com/articles/945735-the-10-GUTsiest-calls-in-nfl-history

race in Cambridge, left the race to take the subway, and rejoined the race not far from the finish line.[72]

I suppose these were GUTsy things to do—risky, dodgy, and dangerous—but they don't fit my definition of true "GUTsiness."

Of course, GUTsy means brave, plucky, and determined—but to me it means more than that. It also means being able to respect yourself. Yes, it does mean getting off your butt and taking those big chances and going after those big GUTsy goals, but it also means listening to your brain, your heart, and your GUT.

A good friend of mine went with some college buddies on spring break to Lake Powell, a massive reservoir on the Colorado River surrounded by high, red sandstone cliffs. The boys decided they'd do some cliff jumping into the water. It looked like fun, but when my friend got to the top of the cliff and looked down into the lake, he realized he didn't know what was under the surface. He knew that Lake Powell is full of hidden crags and boulders that lurk just below the water line, and his GUT all of a sudden felt pretty queasy.

But the guys were shouting at him to go first, so he did. He leaped about 45 feet straight down into the water. Fortunately, he hit no obstacles. But he could have, and that's what shakes him up today when he talks about it. "I could have been paralyzed or killed. My GUT told me it was a dumb, dangerous thing to do. Why did I do it?"

We all know why he did it, because he didn't want to look like a pansy in front of his friends. He wanted to show he was "brave," careless, macho. He wanted to show he was "GUTsy."

To me, that kind of behavior isn't GUTsy. It's just stupid.

Guys who ride motorcycles without helmets, college kids who smoke or binge drink, people who cheat or experiment with

---

72 Givens, Kelsey, "The 20 Dumbest Things Athletes Have Done," BR Bleacher Report, October 18, 2011. http://bleacherreport.com/articles/899492-the-20-dumbest-things-athletes-have-done

drugs or indulge in chancy sexual behavior—this is not "GUTsy." This is stupid.

GUTsy means you do what you can to prepare for the risk before you take it.

You find out if there are rocks under the surface before you take the jump.

Of course, you can't know every possible obstacle that could stop you from taking a risk. You can over-think and over-calculate and never take the risk. If you knew it all, it wouldn't be a risk. Moreover, as Adam Lazarus says, "GUTsy calls don't always work. If they did, they wouldn't be GUTsy."

When it comes right down to it, GUTsy is a matter of character.

It's about discovering your passion and purpose—your "Big Why"—and going for it. It's about listening to that clear message from deep down inside you that tells you what you should be doing with your life.

It's about going for big GUTsy goals that will make a real difference to the people you love and care about, whether those people are your family or your work team or your company or the whole world.

It's about staying up late working because you love your work. It's about flying across the ocean or into space because you've got to know if you can do it. It's about writing that book or getting that degree or starting that business or running that marathon, because you have to or you'll die.

It's about refusing to settle for anything less than a joyful, inspiring, useful life. (It's *not* about "grit," the death march so many of us go through just because we're "supposed" to.)

It's about making the contribution only you can make, because only you have that particular combination of power and smarts and intestinal fortitude to make it.

It's about balancing your brain (intelligence), your heart (passion), and your GUT (inner compass).

It's about taking the risk of loving others. It's about leading them with humility and having the grace to let them take the lead and grow themselves.

It's about huddling with them, engaging with them, winning or losing with them, feeling what they feel even though it's easier to go off and play games on your phone.

It's about taking off, paying the price, and winning every step of the way, remembering that pushing to the failure point is the formula for personal growth and achievement.

It's about *loving* your life.

In the end, it's about the kind of person you are.

So . . . *what kind of person are you?*

AFTERWORD

By Kathy L. Murphy

I met Sam Bracken when I read his first book, *My Orange Duffel Bag.*

I loved that book from the beginning. I learned the story of a boy who made the right choices when people were actively trying to steer him wrong. It was about a horrible childhood of abuse and abandonment, but it was also about hope and faith.

I learned about a boy who was given no chances in life, but who said to himself, "Okay, what are you going to do about it?"

Let me tell you why Sam's story is critically important now.

I've been a youth leader most of my life, involved with kids' camps, church youth group, mission trips, community theater, Girl Scouts—I have done it all. There were always a few dysfunctional kids who needed extra help. In those days dysfunction was abnormal, but now it's the normal thing. It used to be that a few kids had serious problems—now it seems that most of them do. Something is missing—I think it's hope.

I also volunteered at a local mission to teach homeless people how to write their stories. So many of them would look at me, and there was nothing behind their eyes. They couldn't read or write, so I told them, "I'm going to write it for you." Then, as they told their stories, a light would go on in their eyes. And when I would print their stories, and they held their own stories in their hands, that light would come on again for a time. These folks were not just homeless, they were hopeless—but in their own stories, they began to sense that maybe there was some strength inside of them, something that could give them courage.

There's a terrible, growing lack in our society. It's a lack of meaning, a lack of hope. The question is, "What are we going to do about it?"

That's why I love the message Sam Bracken gives in this book: "Yes, life is tough—isn't that great? Joy in life can't be separated from hardship. It takes GUTs to live a great life!" This message is needed more than anything else. It's timeless and for all ages.

Every person will come to a crossroads in life. Too many are deciding to take the road of just giving up. They say, "I can't face it, it's so awful, my life is so bad."

Well, I know a thing or two about challenges. I've been through financial disaster. I've lost a home and a business. I've had three heart operations. I've felt like my life was spinning out of control.

But even though I'm scared to death half the time, I'm fearless. I can't whine about my life. When I come to the crossroads, I refuse to take the road of fear and hopelessness. I choose the road of passion and purpose. I choose the joyful life, and that takes GUTs.

What Sam has discovered in this book is the secret of that kind of life. Now that you've read this book, you're in on the secret. So here's my question: "What are you going to do about it?"

Kathy L. Murphy is the founder of the Pulpwood Queens, the world's largest book club, with some 650 chapters in nearly every U.S. state and fifteen other countries. The club started with six people and now counts tens of thousands of members. Her passion is promoting literacy worldwide. "Books are the diamonds in our tiara," she says, "the treasures we hold in our hands that connect us to each other."

ACKNOWLEDGMENTS

I would like to thank all those in my life who have helped me discover how to use my head, heart, and GUTs to live a full life of power and purpose. I am so grateful for the handful of people who have reached out, reached up, and reached across and helped me—just one person.

My mother lived her life with GUTs, and she taught me how to live my life with GUTs. Thanks, Mom. My wife Kim and my kids, Beau, Ben, Jake, and Hannah, have taught me what it means to live a GUTsy life! They have also been very patient with me over the months we have worked on this manuscript.

I would also like to thank my good friend Dr. Breck England for always challenging my thinking and helping me write this great little book. Breck lives his life with GUTs in his own wonderful way. Breck, I am grateful for your friendship and the faith you have in me.

Special thanks to Coach Bill Curry for writing the foreword and to Kathy Murphy, who wrote the afterword.

AUTHOR BIO

Sam Bracken rose up against impossible odds to live the American dream. He and his wife Kim live happily in the Rocky Mountains with their four children. Thanks to a love of sports and a competitive spirit, he parlayed those skills into a career as an executive with the world's largest leadership training organization, FranklinCovey. After leaving FranklinCovey in early 2016, Sam became the VP of Business Development for Garff Enterprises, a multi-billion dollar automotive group. He travels all over the world speaking on change, leadership and excellence. Sam attained his MBA from the Marriott School of Management and graduated from Georgia Tech with honors. A member of the National Speakers Association, he motivates people toward their highest goals.

My ORANGE DUFFEL BAG
a Journey to Radical Change

CONTACT US @
orangeduffelbag.com

TRAINING

KEYNOTE

My Orange Duffel Bag
Inspire your people as the energetic, passionate Sam Bracken tells the story of his amazing personal transformation from abused child to business leader.

Set Gutsy Goals
COMPETENCY: Goal Execution
Based on the breakthrough book *GUTS!*, learn how to achieve your own gutsy goals—the things you really want to do with your life or your team.

Huddle for Diversity
COMPETENCY: Diversity
Teammates with wildly diverse backgrounds huddle on the field and combine their strengths to win. Learn how to leverage diversity in your organization through the power of the huddle. Focus on the things that unite, instead of dividing people into categories.

Lead from the GUT
COMPETENCY: Leadership
It's not a title that makes you a leader—it's GUTS! In this course, develop the character, the goals, the skills, and the tools of a gutsy leader who leads a winning team.

The Orange Duffel Bag
COMPETENCY: Personal Transformation
Based on the classic book about Sam Bracken's remarkable personal transformation, learn how to transform your own life or organization, no matter what the obstacles may be.

"Change is hard. Everyone wants it. So few get it. Sam lays out a fool-proof, step-by-step approach to change through sharing his own remarkable journey from victim to conqueror."

Stephen R. Covey,
Author of The *7 Habits of Highly Effective People*